CONQUEROR OF A SHATTERED HEART

TIFFANY ITOBORE

ISBN 9780578750859

CONTENT

PREFACE

When a bowl is broken in Japan, rather than being thrown away, it is put back together with the cracks being filled with gold to create a beautiful lining. Amazing, isn't it? This emphasizes the fact that a life shattered by terrible circumstances is not useless. In other words, we must embrace our pains, sorrows, flaws and imperfections so that we can create a beautiful piece of art in ourselves. It's the same way broken tiles are used to make beautiful designs. Besides, if delicious meals can be made from bitter leaves, then why can't you make a beautiful story out of your supposed terrible circumstance?

If you are reading this, then it means you still believe in yourself. God hasn't condemned you, so you should not give in to despair. As a matter of fact, God never allows more than what we can bear because He wants us to emerge as conquerors. So, whatever challenge you are facing, you are capable of overcoming it. Just because a few dirty drops get into an ocean doesn't make it dirty. Likewise, don't let your bad experiences make you think your life is horrible.

Reflecting on my life, I was denied by my father, discarded and sold out by my mother, maltreated by my guardians, molested by a counsellor and betrayed by my spouse. In fact, if there's one word that described my life, it would be miserable. Not even the depths of your imagination can decipher the extent of my suffering. No doubt, life is full of victims, but it is also full of victors. Through it all, God intervened, and I wrestled till I snatched victory from the jaws of defeat. I could have been a victim when life happened to me, but I chose to become a victor.

Conqueror of a Shattered Heart is the story of an individual who, despite being shattered by life, chose to put back the broken pieces of her life with cracks filled with gold in order to create a beautiful lining. You think your life is broken beyond repair? This book will shatter such belief.

Chapter 1

~~Normal~~ Not Normal

"Was there even such a thing as normal? People had terrible things behind their faces sometimes. He knew that now."

-Stephen King, Hearts in Atlantis

If I had to sum up my childhood in just two words, I'd say: "Not normal!" I was born at seven months. When I appeared, everyone was gutted at my form because a new baby ought to be embraced with both hands, but I was so minute that a palm was enough to contain me. That's not normal! More disturbing is the fact that, while folks rejoice at a new-born baby's first cry, mine was different.

How do I know this? I never knew my father, and as I write this, I am yet to lock eyes with him. Not because he is dead at least not while I write this but he abandoned me, feeling I was a misfortune. As for my mother, she was present in the delivery room simply because I was trapped in her womb as all her efforts to eliminate me prior to my due date were to no avail. Could that be normal?

Without question, I was deprived of love and parental care, which made my childhood a nightmare from which I am still trying to wake. Though I've known several other men with my mother who became my stepfathers, it still appeared as if I wasn't destined to have a father figure because none of them ever attempted to fill my dad's shoes.

To make matters worse, my mother, who should have filled the void, despised me with a passion such that she would often beat me and do wicked things to me for reasons I couldn't fathom. Sometimes, her attitude made me question if she was, in fact, my biological mother because she had not even an iota of love for me.

The mere sight of me irritated my mother. Did he adopt me? Was my conception a product of rape? Does she hate me because she couldn't abort me or because I reminded her of my father? These questions lurked in my mind as I was buried in turmoil. Accordingly, being raised by a mother who never wanted me was just short of devastating.

I endured so much suffering that I even questioned why God brought me into this world through such a dysfunctional family. Why did God have to lie? Yes, you heard me right! After all, He said, "Though my father and mother forsake me, He the LORD will receive me." Yet, He also abandoned me ... maybe because I wasn't normal.

I grew up in an old, ugly house filled with roaches. We hardly had it cleaned, so everywhere was full of filth and rats. The only time it was clean was when I cleaned it myself. Needless to say, as young as six, I already bore all the household tasks. First, I had to wake up early every morning ahead of everyone Ma, Don (my stepdad) and my siblings, Joshua and Krissy to get their clothes ready for the day. I never questioned why, at the crack of dawn, I'd have to walk into a dark room that nobody used at the back of the house and sift through a huge pile of clothes. Maybe it was just my punishment for being an unwanted child. The pile was always bigger than me, requiring a lot of energy and time to find what was suitable.

After that, I would iron all the clothes, lay them out nicely, clean the entire house and do all the other chores before having the time to fend for myself. To be frank, most mornings, I wouldn't eat because, after sorting everyone out and going on to prepare myself, breakfast would have already been served and eaten. So, I often went to school on an empty stomach if I even went to school at all. This was the routine every single day of the week. Don't even mention the weekends, they were worse!

Without the completion of my chores, I had no right to food or even sleep. I remember one time I returned from school and decided to take a nap. Ma returned from work and started questioning me, "Have you washed the dishes, why didn't you sweep that damn trash out of the door?" As she talked to me, I kept dozing off because I was really exhausted from school. As a result, she hit me with a belt, telling me that if I wanted to go to sleep or even eat, I must complete my chores first.

On top of that, I was restricted to eating just once a day. Nonetheless, what I despised the most was that it was always something out of a can. I would be subjected to a can of beans while the rice and chicken or the other goodies in the refrigerator were usually reserved for others because I wasn't worthy of eating proper food in my own home. Let me astound you even further: to even drink water from the kitchen sink was a privilege because I usually had to drink mine from the bathroom faucet, and if Ma caught me in the act, she would beat the hell out of me. What was I supposed to do? I had no access to clean water like the others.

I felt like a slave in my own home, and in no time, I was became conditioned to see these anomalies as normal. In my mind, little kids like me do not eat adult food, but then again, Josh and Krissy were given proper food and care. So, why was my case different? Was it just the fact that I wasn't normal? I could not tell. In any case, I couldn't wait to become an adult so I could eat adult food like grits, eggs, toast and bacon like everyone else.

I loved and always yearned to go to school, not because I fancied education but because it was the only place I ate proper food. I'd first noticed that the food at school tasted differently and was better than the canned food Ma gave me all the time. Although, sometimes, she'd try to make the peas taste different by adding salt or pepper, but it never helped. I had gotten tired of the cardboard taste and would only eat just enough to satisfy my hunger. Nonetheless, food wasn't the only thing I loved about school; I also loved my teachers because they were so different from Ma. They were friendly and caring, especially Ms. Shine who took a keen interest in me.

Unfortunately, the joy at school always ended the moment I returned to my prison cell at home. I hated boarding the school bus because it was so noisy and hot. No one talked to me because they had no interest in me. The other kids on the bus would always give me this weird look and then whisper into each other's ears, making a mockery of me. I would always hear things like, "Why is she always wearing dirty clothes? Why does her hair look like that?" As a matter of fact, Ma would often deliberately make me wear dirty clothes to school so that I could be an object of mockery.

Whenever I heard them mocking me, I would crouch down in the sticky school bus seat a little lower so that the kids would just forget I existed. It didn't matter though because, day after day, I had to cope with this till I got off the bus. What choice did I have? While the other kids were always so eager to get home to meet their parents, I wasn't because I knew I was going to be met with house chores which had to be completed before Ma returned or I'd get spanked.

One fateful day, Ms. Shine asked, "Tiffany, does your mom help you practice your words every night?" I was perplexed because no one at home paid me any attention, let alone practiced words with me. Didn't Ms. Shine know that mommies don't have the time to help their kids with schoolwork? I immediately recalled the last time I asked Ma to help me with my homework: "You betta get that shit out of my face!" I didn't know what to tell Ms. Shine, so I kept mute. Ms. Shine then gave me some books to take home for my mom or dad to read to me.

I knew that wouldn't happen because Ma never cared about me, and Don treated me like she did a slave. We never had any interactions except when he wanted to accuse me of something or ask me annoying questions like, "What the fuck are you looking at?" or "Why did you take my honey bun from the table?" I often tried to avoid him. He was worse than Ma because he often relished in frustrating me, knowing my mum would always take his side. He always acted as though he was competing with me for Ma's attention. Nonetheless, I took the assignment home, wanting to give them the benefit of a doubt.

When school ended that day, I clutched the plastic bag Ms. Shine had given me and ran to my bus stop. When I got home and had finished my chores, I thought about the books and wondered how I would show them to Ma. After much consideration, I decided that I would wait till dinner was over when she would be relaxed. Soon after, I heard the sound of the TV blaring in the living room while

Ma and Don were laughing.

It was late, and I had already given Krissy a bath and put her to bed. So, I walked into the living room and stood by the door. My stomach rumbled a little as I noticed them sharing a tub of vanilla ice cream while their eyes were glued to the screen, enjoying the programme. As I turned to return to my room where I shared a bed with Joshua and Krissy, Ma caught me.

"Tiffany, what the hell are you still doing up?" she asked. Words failed me because I knew I was supposed to be in bed, but I needed to practice my words. "Didn't you hear me? I said, 'What are you still doing awake?'"

Then I spoke up, "Ms. Shine wants you to read with me." I shakily held up the book.

"Girl, if you don't get your ass in bed, it's gonna be a problem," she replied. A solid lump formed in my throat. Ms. Shine would be upset with me if I didn't practice reading my words. So, I stood still.

"What did I just tell you?" Ma asked, with anger starting to lace her voice.

"To go to bed," I responded.

"Then get your ass in that bed," she said.

I stared at her with tears beginning to form in the corners of my eyes. I knew she wasn't busy so I couldn't understand why she didn't want to assist me. I looked at Don. His eyes were still glued to the television as though he heard nothing. Maybe he would be willing to read to me, I thought.

"Don, can you read this to me?" I asked.

Before I knew what was happening, Ma dashed to where I was and struck me hard on the face. For seconds, my vision turned white and blue. Then I staggered back, hitting the corner of the wall. The book in my hand dropped to the floor as I held my face staring at Ma in horror.

"What the fuck did I just tell you? I just told you to carry your black ass to bed and you are asking if Don could read to you! Ms. Shine doesn't run shit in this house! Take your goddamn ass to bed like I told you to," she yelled.

Like lightning, I bolted back to the room, turned the light off and got into bed. As soon as my head hit the pillow, the hot tears that formed in the corners of my eyes fell down my face. At that point, I knew my education was of no concern to Ma. Good thing the government provided free education for public schools, otherwise, I wonder what my fate would have been.

Luckily, it was the weekend, so that gave me ample time to figure out a response for Ms. Shine. Most weekends, Krissy's dad would come pick her up to spend time with him over the weekend. This always left a sour taste in my mouth as I often felt jealous that my sister was lucky to have her dad always come for her when I didn't even know who mine was, let alone be able to visit him.

Unlike weekdays, when I still got a can of something to eat after completing my chores, I would literally be neglected, barely eating something substantial till Monday. Sometimes, I even wondered if Ma breastfed me when I was a toddler because, with such attitude from her, I doubt if I ever had a taste of her breast milk.

From my room, I would perceive all kinds of delicacies such as oxtail with cabbage and others coming from the kitchen, and the aroma would make my hunger pangs even worse. I would wonder what Krissy was eating while away with her dad. Whatever it was, I knew it was far better than drinking tap water just to make the hunger holes go away. On one occasion, I thought about asking Ma for food, but after what happened with the homework, I dared not. So, most weekends, I went to bed without eating.

Monday arrived, and by this time, Krissy had returned home for the week. So, I got up as usual to get everyone's clothes ready. The only thing different was that my hunger pangs had gotten worse. I felt nauseous. I wanted to puke, but there was nothing inside me to do so with except for my lungs, liver and intestine. If I didn't eat something right then and there, I was certainly going to pass out. Since everyone was still asleep, I snuck into the kitchen and opened the refrigerator. I was surprised to see a white Styrofoam box from the night before sitting on a rack. I peeked over my shoulder before opening it. Most of the oxtail was eaten, but a few pieces remained, along with some white rice.

Without hesitation, I dipped my hand, scooped out some rice and stuffed it quickly into my mouth. My stomach groaned upon doing so, and I looked around again for fear that someone may have heard it. I stuffed a few more pieces of cold, hard oxtail in my mouth. Afterwards, I closed the box, put it back into the refrigerator and left instantly so that Ma and Don wouldn't find out my little secret. At least my pain would stop till lunch at school restores life back to me.

I returned to my room to grab my books. I figured I would just tell Ms. Shine that Ma was busy. I certainly couldn't tell her that I was beaten for seeking parental guidance, even though it left a bruise on my face. I tried practicing the words, though I knew I wasn't doing it well. Still, I kept at it, hoping that I could learn some of the words before I got to school that morning.

Again, it didn't matter because it looked like I wasn't going to school that day as no one had gotten up yet. Sighing, I stood up and walked to the bedroom I shared with my siblings. It was no use trying to nudge Joshua because the only person who could get him to wake up was Ma and she herself wasn't awake.

Eager to go to school that morning, I walked to Ma's bedroom door and knocked. No one answered, so I knocked again. I hoped that she wouldn't get mad. Just as I was about to knock a third time, the door swung open and Don stepped out asking what I wanted. I explained that I needed Ma to wake up so I could go to school but he interrupted, saying she wasn't awake. Unmoved by this, I tried to peek into the room, but he pushed me back, reiterating that she wasn't awake.

The bottom line was, I wasn't going to make it to school that day, as I predicted. I loved school because it was my only salvation from prison, and I hated when I missed my only opportunity to leave. I couldn't find a sensible reason why I didn't go that day. Maybe Ma was still pissed that I asked her to read to me. After all, she didn't speak to me all through the weekend, except when she instructed me to sweep the kitchen.

I returned to my room disappointed, longing for the next opportunity to go to school. The next day, I woke up hungry as usual. I think I fell asleep even before dinner the night before. However, I had no time to think about food because I had to get everyone's clothes ready before they woke up. I tried to take my mind off of school so I wouldn't become disappointed again if I didn't make it.

Luckily, I made it to school that day. Nevertheless, I left on an empty belly, and by the time I arrived at school, the pain had become unbearable. Although I'd gotten to school early enough to eat something, it was just cereal, and my stomach wouldn't hold out until I had lunch. I was jealous of all the other kids in my classroom as they brought their own lunch from home. I wondered what kind of dinner they had at night. Was it like my canned food? Oh, lest I forget, I mostly went to sleep hungry. It was at this point that I decided I wouldn't go hungry anymore.

At lunch time, I quietly got up and walked to the back of the classroom where my classmates' backpacks were neatly kept. Some of them had lunchboxes while some didn't. I peeked around to make sure no one was watching. When the coast was clear, I turned and opened the first backpack I saw. I took the ham and cheese sandwich in it and hid it underneath my shirt. Instantly, shame burned my face, but perpetual starvation had made me adopt stealing as a habit.

I ended up doing this everyday—that is, until I got caught. I guess I had become addicted to it so much that I didn't realize Ms. Shine had been getting complaints from the other kids that their lunch was always going missing. On the day of reckoning, Ms. Shine asked me to remain inside for recess instead of going out to play.

"Tiffany, do you know why you're in trouble?" she asked.

I looked down at my feet as I didn't have the heart to look at her.

"Tiffany, look at me," she said firmly.

I looked at her.

"Tiffany, you've been taking food that doesn't belong to you. Why?" she asked.

I couldn't tell her because that would mean trouble with Ma. She waited a few minutes before speaking again.

"Tiffany, what's wrong? You have been acting weird, and now you are stealing food. Why?" Seeing my remorseful face, she continued, "Tiffany, I will bring you food if you're hungry, but I'm going to have to tell your mom that you've been acting out, okay?"

Oh, my goodness! My heart froze for a second. Ma mustn't hear about this. I didn't mean to misbehave but I had been so hungry that I couldn't concentrate in class. Tears began streaming down my face. Ms. Shine was disappointed, and now Ma would be too. Why is my life this abnormal? Or was this normal too? Though I was now seven, I still had no right to ask questions in the house.

Yet, there were lots of questions that burned the core of my chest: "Who is my father? Where was he? What would he say about all of this? Would I get to experience a 'normal' life with my dad like my sister did with hers?" I needed to know who he was, what his name was, if I looked like him and why he was never around. I needed to know everything—everything I didn't know. I was lonely and dying inside because of it.

The only other person I knew as family apart from Ma was my Grandma. She was Ma's mother and, though I didn't visit her much, we often spoke over the phone. Now, I never had a real conversation with Ma, but with Grandma, I sure did. She always inquired to know how I coped and, though sometimes I told her I was okay, most times I shared my plight with her. I knew Grandma yearned to spend more time with me or possibly come to get me, but because she lived in a different city, it was difficult.

However, she kept promising to do so at her earliest convenience. Whenever I heard this, it rekindled my hopes for a better life. I imagined Grandma was a queen in a castle that would someday rescue me from the evil monsters I lived with.

As a pastor in a church, the love of God was portrayed in her voice that I always relished talking to her.

Overtime, my behavior at school kept getting worse. I was constantly getting in trouble and I couldn't understand why. All I knew was that my life was ravaged by so much hurt and it played out in my attitude and behavior at school. As a result, Ma often came to school to see my teacher. Every time she came, all hell would break loose at night. Ma was never tired of beating and whatever she hit me with left marks and bruises on my skin. Though she could use anything she laid her hands on, the extension cord was her favorite.

On one occasion, talking to her almost cost me my life. I had decided that I was going to inform Grandma that I was keen to leave home and go on to live with her instead, but I couldn't call her when Ma and Don were around, especially to tell her this. So, one day, as I returned from school before Ma and Don, I ran to my room, took off my shoes and grabbed the cordless phone.

I didn't want to be caught with it in case they came home early, so I went to the back room of the house where all the clothes were and closed myself in the closet. No one was going to see me in there because no one hardly came to that room— except me.

I dialed Grandma's digits, but she didn't pick up. I started freaking out. I dialed a second time and still got no response. This was a rare opportunity and, shockingly, Grandma wasn't picking up. I tried again and, at that point, I was ready to give up since I got no response. I decided to try one last time and, surprisingly, she picked up the phone. Immediately, I choked back tears. I didn't know why I wanted to cry all of a sudden, perhaps the sound of her voice comforted me. I wanted to leave the house so badly and go live with her because she was the only one who could rescue me.

I begged her to come and get me, but she refuted, saying she needed time to fix some things. Still, I insisted, telling her how badly I was treated, and though she acknowledged my situation, she only promised to come for me when she was ready. My expectations were dashed, and I wanted to cry because if Grandma couldn't come and get me right then, all hopes were lost. Just then, I heard a sound right outside of the closet door. I sat still, holding my breath. I wasn't in the room alone! Someone knew that I was in the closet and was coming towards it.

Before I could tell Grandma that I had to go and hang up, the closet door swung open. My heart raced in my chest as I looked right into Don's eyes. I was so paralyzed by fear feeling he already knew who I was talking to and the sickening smirk on his face. What happened next, I wish I could forget, but my memory tends to replay it every time as if it happened yesterday. It started with a slap on my face. I fell backwards screaming.

Surprisingly, a spirit possessed me with the courage to slap him back. I was fed up! And that's how Don and I wrestled, but as a full-grown man, I was no match for him. So, he kept hitting me hard. Luckily, Grandma was on the line and, by that time, she was screaming my name, asking what was happening. Don kept punching me, but I wouldn't give up fighting back.
Suddenly, he grabbed the phone, and called Ma to inform her of what I did, and in no time, Ma arrived. She must have already been on her way home because she showed up way too fast. Ma's eyes cut me like razor blades, and with no further ado, Ma's fists were on me too. I felt every bit of her anger on me. Her punches were like jagged knives that cut everything I had in me—my heart, my life, my spirit.

Why? I was her child—her flesh and blood. I couldn't understand why she wouldn't even give me the chance to plead my case. I couldn't understand how a mother would choose to listen to her lover over her biological child. Despite the physical abuse, she was willing to further crush me. I shut my eyes tightly, tears squeezing out, straining against the reality that I was going to die there. I thought to myself, this is just not normal.

Pain can be a gift or a curse. In my case, it was both. My pain was a gift because it awakened me to the harsh realities of life. On the other hand, it was a curse because the cruel nature of this world began with my own mother. Mothers would naturally protect their children from pain and danger, but mine not only exposed me to it, she was, in fact, the pain in my ass. Unlike mothers, Ma hated me, and she seemed to like it. She enjoyed seeing me in the depths of agony. Why was it just me? After all, she had it easy on Josh and Krissy. I drowned in confusion as I slept that night.

Suddenly, a slap on my head awakened me back to reality. "Get your ass up before I knock the shit out of you," Ma yelled. I was still physically hurt from the battering I had received the previous night, and even worse, I was emotionally hurt. Groggily, I sat up, fearful of what she might do next if I did not respond. It was morning and I went straight to the back room to gather everyone's clothes. I knew that I wouldn't have time to do anything else except get Josh and Krissy's clothes ready, so I had to go to school with what I was wearing: a dirty t-shirt and a pair of pink shorts the same thing I'd worn all weekend; the same thing I was wearing when Ma and Don beat me up in the closet; the same shirt that was wrinkled and torn when the police officer questioned me.

Oh yeah, the police came to the house later that day. Grandma called them after she heard what was happening on the other end of the phone. However, they left in no time after Ma and Don denied mistreating me. They just told the officer that I had gotten a spanking for disobedience. Though the officer inquired from me if it was true, and as much as I wanted to reveal the truth, I concurred for peace to reign.

They say the most unbearable pain in the world is to be burnt alive while the next is the labor women go through during childbirth, yet every mother has to go through this for her child. A mother's love is the strongest in the world next to God's. A mother would do anything for her child. If need be, she may even take her own life so that her child may live. More so, a mad woman, even in her insanity, would always care for and protect her child.

My mother was obviously not insane or a lunatic. Yet, she was diametrically opposed to everything a true mother should be. Allow me to astound you even further: you couldn't rate her love for me as the weakest. In point of fact, it was non-existent because she felt nothing in her heart for me. Not love, not empathy, not care or even mercy. Needless to say, my life was shattered from childhood. This is not normal.

Chapter 2

DESERTED!

"The biggest disease today is not leprosy or tuberculosis but rather the feeling of being unwanted, uncared for and deserted by everybody."
-Mother Teresa

When the police officer came to the house, the bruises from the beatings I got were not visible, but by the time I got to school a day later, they were so evident. Both of my arms were covered with dark purple spots and my right eye also had a bruise below it. The kids on the bus and in my class had noticed the marks on me because they kept staring as if I were a monster with two heads. In fact, when Mrs. Shine saw me, she reacted as though she had seen a ghost.

Throughout the entire reading lesson that morning, she kept an eye on me like a hawk. Eventually, she asked how I got the bruises on my arms and face and, as usual, I became dumb, scared of her reaction. Though I didn't answer her verbally, I knew she would dig out the truth. Then Ma and Don would find out and my vicious cycle of pain would begin again. So, after much persistence, I had no choice than to let the cat out of the bag. Ms. Shine was astounded, wondering how on earth a real mother would do this to a child she labored for.

Nonetheless, she patted me on the shoulder and asked me to go eat my lunch before walking away. For the rest of that day at school, I did my work, trying not to compound issues so Ma didn't get any call that day. On one occasion, I had taken a bad mood to school as a result of my hunger and unhappiness and, as such, I didn't want to listen to anything Ms. Shine or anyone had to say. Carlos, the boy who sat beside me, had taken my pencil and I slapped him for it.

I felt bad for acting that way, but I couldn't help it. The news got to Ma, and later that night, she took the telephone cord out of the wall and whipped me with it. As a punishment, I was deprived of food that night. I also couldn't eat the food Ms. Shine packed for me. Although it was under the jacket on the floor of my room, Ma had dared me to get out of my bed. Out of fear, I slept in hunger.

On a certain day, I was preparing for school in the morning as usual and I was really starving and couldn't take it anymore. I may just die any moment, I thought. So, I decided that I was going to steal some food from the refrigerator to just survive. It was in that process of trying to feed myself from the crumbs that fell off my mother's table that I got caught. What happened next is still a shock to me. It was like the day of reckoning!

Ma got a belt and began to beat me ruthlessly. To this day, I cannot tell if she actually knew that she was whipping me with the buckle of the belt because, in retrospect, I still find it to be inhumane. However, in reality, that was what happened, and I yelled at the top of my voice, but she continued regardless. Luckily, the school bus arrived, and the driver honked the horn. With rage, she yelled, "Get out of my house! Get out of my house!" I ran out to join the school bus, making my narrow escape. Otherwise, I may have given up the ghost that day.

Once I sat down and the school bus moved, everyone began to stare at me in a weird manner, but I thought it was merely because of my tears. Soon after, I was so exhausted from the beating that I became dizzy and drifted off. I tried to steal some food because I was hungry but now, my hunger was no longer the issue, my pain was! When the bus arrived at school, I woke up instantly and got down, heading to my class. As soon as my teacher laid eyes on me, she was gutted and instantly inquired what had happened to me that caused the flow of blood. Really? Was I bleeding? I was puzzled because I wasn't even aware of it.

When my teacher continued to insist that my right eye was bleeding, I touched the side of my face and felt the fresh blood drying up. I was stunned that Ma busted my eye and I didn't even know it. At that instant, the pain became conscious and I screamed, "Ouch!" However, I knew with that, I owed my teacher an explanation. I quickly came up with a lie that I had fallen down the staircase accidentally, but she wouldn't buy my flimsy excuse. She had overlooked my mum's behavior previously, but this time, she wouldn't.

Before I knew it, the intercom came on in the classroom and a message from the front office left a message for Ms. Shine to send me to the front office with all my things. I was shocked! We seldom got calls requiring kids to report to the front office. What was wrong? Surprisingly, Ms. Shine gave her consent. As I walked down to the front office, a lot of thoughts crossed my mind. When I got there, the principal, Mrs. Vander, told me to wait in a chair.

Afterwards, I learned that an institution called The Department of Children and Families was contacted and they dashed down to my school to investigate the situation. After interrogating me and then contacting Ma, she was found guilty as she had told a different story from mine. At that juncture, my teacher pulled me to a corner and started to cry, confessing how much she cared for me. I was so moved that I had to reveal the truth. The consequence: I was doomed for the group home.

Later on, as they drove me down to only God-knows-where, my mind continued to ponder. Would Ma be mad at me? Would she dread my absence? I had a funny feeling that she wouldn't even miss me. She probably felt happy that I had been taken away. Upon arriving at the group home, I realized that it was for girls who were much older than I was. Perhaps that was the best option at the time.

The place appeared to be like a home, only a lot different from mine. It smelled better and roaches weren't crawling up the walls. At the entrance, a woman sat behind a desk where I got checked in. My heart began to beat fast as I was ushered through the dark hallway. Around the corner was a small kitchen and table.

The lady asked me to sit at the table and wait until my food was ready. Though I was hungry, my brain couldn't stop wondering if I was going to spend the rest of my life there. I folded my arms on top of the table and laid my head in them. A tear escaped my eye as I watched Ms. Angie take a frozen meal out of the freezer and put it in the microwave. I had mixed feelings. I was being treated special in a place that wasn't my home, and on the other hand, I did not know my fate from there. After pressing the buttons, she left the kitchen.

After dinner, I continued to ponder. I didn't like living with Ma and Don, but that didn't make this new place any better because it felt weird. Later when I got into my room, everything seemed awkward. I was lying on a bed that wasn't mine and wearing a shirt that didn't belong to me. I was so cold because the vent in the ceiling was right above where I slept, and the blanket I had over me wasn't thick enough. I wished Krissy was with me. At least sleeping with her would have felt warmer and better. Part of me wanted to sneak out and return to Ma to apologize. Another part of me just wanted to escape and go somewhere else entirely.

As I pondered, I fell asleep. Later that night, some girls at the group home pounced on me and started hitting me with pillows. I couldn't fight back because they were much older. Eventually, they eloped with all my things. I was in awe! It was as though witches had come to torment me. What world have I found myself in? Luckily, the next day I was moved to a new group home for my age bracket.

Somehow, I found a way to call my mum to explain my plight to her. I dreaded my life away from home because I didn't feel welcome there; besides, it was a weird place that I wasn't ready to get accustomed to. More so, I'd rather endure the abuse I was used to than the one I wasn't. However, it took a whole month for her to come get me. Ma was asked to take some mandatory classes before she was allowed to take me back, which she did.

Since Ma had gone through the trouble to meet all the requirements to reclaim me, I felt she would turn a new leaf. At least, she would have felt the pain of being deserted like me. So, I returned home hoping to start fresh and enjoy a mother's true love, but sadly, her attitude did not change, neither was she remorseful. Rather, she only became craftier. My heart was broken!

I was taken aback. So, I wondered why Ma would go through all the stress if all she wanted me back for was to cause me more suffering because when I returned, she resorted to verbal abuses such that her words made me feel so worthless and hopeless. I felt so cursed that I began to wonder who my father was. I only knew my mother who took pleasure in making my life a living hell. What about my father? Would he treat me this way too? Who was he? What did he look like? Would he be happy seeing me suffer like this? I became increasingly anxious to find out, so I decided to ask Ma.

Although my heart sped up in my small chest whilst thinking about it, I planned to ask Ma when she was in a good mood and when Don wasn't around because I had noticed she acted quite differently in his absence. One Sunday morning, I figured it was the best time to ask since she had just returned from church and church service seemed to make her happy. So, I waited patiently until she changed her clothes into something more comfortable. Knowing Don would be coming home soon with his beer from the corner store, I hurried into her room.

"Hey, Ma, can I ask you something?"
"What?" she said.
"Who is my daddy?" I asked after taking a deep breath.
I looked away briefly before making eye contact with her again.
"Huh?" she said, sounding confused.
"Do I have a daddy? Who is my daddy?"
The small frown that was on Ma's face got bigger. I couldn't tell if she was mad or confused, but I knew that I caught her off guard.
"What do you want to know that for?"
"B-B-because I've never seen him before."
"Well, maybe that's for a reason," Ma said with a rising tone. "I have nothing to do with that. Don't ask me nothing 'bout that nigga! What are you asking me about his sorry ass for?"

I was speechless.
"Move! get the f*** out of my way!" she yelled, pushing me against the wall as she walked to the kitchen. I was confused. I couldn't understand why she didn't want me to ask her about him.

"...asking me about that motherfucker! Carry your ass in that room and sit your damn ass down somewhere," She continued to yell from the kitchen. I ran into the room. "And don't bring your ass out that room for the rest of the day!" She added.

She continued with her cuss words, saying that I wouldn't finish high school or amount to anything. I was locked inside crying and regretting having asked about my father in the first place. The next morning came too soon. I woke up hungry and tired. Hungry because I did not eat anything the night before, and tired from crying all night. I was somewhat fed up living in the house.

I wondered if I could follow Krissy to her dad's house since I didn't know where mine was. Maybe the next time he came to pick her up, I would ask if I could go with them. During this time, I soaked my bed with tears, praying every single night, looking at the sky and wishing upon a star for a miracle to happen.

I strongly believed that wishes came to pass. So, I would pray and pray, and though nothing changed, I didn't stop believing. Soon after, I wrote a handwritten letter to Ma, apologizing for all my misdeeds. Though I felt innocent, I just wanted peace to reign at home, and even more, I wanted love between us. If her motherly love had a price tag, I was willing to pay the grand price.

A few days later, I woke up with everything normal as I did my chores, then left for school. After school, I returned to find the house locked. Normally when that happened, I would just wait till someone came home. However, when hours passed by and no one showed up, I became worried, wondering what was happening. As an afterthought, I started checking all the windows till I found one that was erroneously left open.

As I got into the house through the window, I noticed that the house was empty. I could only find trash bags around, and while I pondered on what was wrong, I heard a knock on the door. Thank goodness! Ma was back, I thought, feeling relieved. To my amazement, it was someone from the DCF. Why them again?! I was still trying to connect the dots when the representative informed me that Ma had relocated, and I was now a property of DCF, so she had come to take me.

I couldn't decipher what that meant but since no one was home and everywhere was looking desolate, I later decided to go with her hoping that Ma would come and get me later.

However, this time, things happened differently at DCF as they began to take pictures of me including my thumbprints and every piece of information they could get. They ended up placing me in one room with three other girls. When I probed further, I was told that, earlier that day, Ma had visited, informing them that she was fed up and she didn't want me anymore. In Florida, when a parent doesn't want her child anymore, she can give up her rights as a mother. How ridiculous!

I mean, how possible could that be? I couldn't comprehend the information. For a while, I had been well-behaved myself except when I asked about my dad a few days ago. Was she mad at me for that? I didn't want to believe it was true, so I requested to speak to my mum. When Ma answered the call, I burst into tears, asking her if it was true that she had given me up, but she shunned me, saying that she would call me back. I remember crying over the phone, begging my mum not to hang up or leave me, but still, she hung up the phone and that was the end. I was so devastated!

I was later informed that Ma had moved to Georgia and that was why the house was empty, and though Ma had three of us: Josh, Krissy and I, I was the only one she gave up. That's how a new chapter of my life started—being deserted! How could my mother do this to me? How could she give up her first fruit? What exactly was my offence? At first, I had anger issues and behavioral problems because I was abandoned, lonely and I felt so hurt about it. I had been enduring the trauma of not having a dad and then, my mother, my only companion and source of hope decided to give up on me too.

As a kid, I was emotionally pained. Being resigned to a place I never wanted to be, and the thought that my own biological mother could reject me cut me like a knife. I shed tears as I write this… The group home had about thirteen of us in the same situation. Hurt! Broken! Deserted! As a result, we all reacted bitterly, doing terrible things.

Although, the officials painted this pretty picture of how the system was better and how I would be loved and cared for, it was not enough to fill up the void that my mother left when she quitted on me. It was as though my life had fallen like a pack of cards.

Even worse is the fact that life wasn't as they portrayed it to be at the group home as we suffered a whole lot. The staff were fond of mistreating us. They would deprive us of some goodies in the fridge by locking it up, limit us to certain privileges at the group home and speak to us as if we were worthless. As a result, we reacted negatively by transferring aggression on each other every day. Sometimes, we would fight one another for no reason at all because we obviously had mental health problems.

In fact, the staff members would sometimes be the ones to trigger or plan the fights amongst us. I mean, they literally enjoyed watching us fight like it was a TV show to them. For example, the staff could take our things and lie that a particular person was the culprit just to ensure that we confronted one another. Then when it gets horrible, they would begin to talk down on us: "Y'all just stupid, y'all nothing."

So much verbal abuse in the group home that it kept reminding me of how Ma mistreated me. People who were hired to make up for the love and care that we lacked at home happened to be the worst set of people. One would think they knew we were broken and hurt and as such, they would try to be caretakers by filling the voids in our lives. However, 70 percent of them only applied for the job for the money. They were nothing but wolves in sheep's clothing. Hence, I saw the world through my lens as an awful place to be because I endured discomfort not only within my home but even out there in the world.

I hated every moment in the group home, but since I had no other place to go, I accepted my fate. Fortunately, after some time, Grandma found out about my situation and came to claim me at the group home. I was so exhilarated. At long last! Nevertheless, my time with her was short-lived because she also started nagging that she couldn't handle me due to her health. The truth was that she was so impatient with me. After all, if there wasn't an option at all and I had no one except her, she would have kept me, nonetheless.

Due to my terrible upbringing, coupled with my experience at the group home, I started exhibiting some bad attitudes, and Grandma was unempathetic. She instantly concluded that I was toxic and would often call me an evil child. Sometimes, she would pray and try to cast away my demons. On one occasion, there was a party next door and I sneaked out to attend even when she warned me not to.

A few months later, she sent me back to the group home. Ma had dumped me; father was nowhere to be found and the only person in the world I thought would accept me also denied me to my face. At that point, it dawned on me that I was now an orphan. How depressing!

Subsequently, due to our behavioral problems at the group home, we were required to have medical assessment for possible healthcare needs, environmental changes (e.g., different roommates) and periodic counseling. Hence, I had to visit a therapist on a regular basis to aid my growth and healing process. I was assigned to a white man called Mr. Steve. He was quite big and cocky, and I often went to his office for counselling.

Steve would often make me laugh so I could feel comfortable with him, and it worked. Sometimes, he would give me a peck on my cheek, and I would feel weird. Overtime, since no one gave me the kind of attention he did, I felt loved. One day, while I went for therapy in his office, he quickly went to the door, locked it and pounced on me. As a 13-year-old kid, I couldn't comprehend what was happening, but before I knew it, he had stripped off my clothes and sexually abused me. Afterwards, he told me it had to be a secret.

Though he took advantage of me, taking my virginity at that innocent age, I still didn't understand the implications. Yet, every time I went there, he would continue to molest me. One day, a colleague of his, an African American guy, caught him in the act, and though he looked shocked, he kept it to himself and did not raise an alarm.

With that, I thought there was nothing wrong with it, until one day when he took me in his car and had sex with me again. As we drove off, some cops stopped us for a check and, out of curiosity, they decided to take me for examination at a rape center. There and then, they confirmed that I had been sexually molested because his semen was found in me.

Instantly, the cops beat him mercilessly and arrested him. I was bewildered because I couldn't comprehend what was happening or what offence he had committed. Before I knew it, everything went viral and it came up in the news. As a result, Mr. Steve lost his license and was sent to jail. To date, I haven't heard a word about him.

Life is so full of mess. Once again, I was abused by someone who was supposed to care for me. Nonetheless, I blame no one other than my family, for, if they had diligently played their roles in my life, I may never have been exposed to these things at such a tender age. Unlike other kids, I wasn't demanding gifts or luxury, all I wanted was love from the people I call family and yet, I never had it. Rather, I was deprived of it and left deserted.

Chapter 3

PIECE BY PIECE

"A jug fills drop by drop."
-Buddha

Piece by piece, it appeared my life was deteriorating, and sequel to that incident, I was transferred to another group home as they tried to change my environment, hoping it would protect my image and aid my recovery. I also got assigned a new therapist, only this time, it was a female. However, this meant nothing because the group home was a toxic, painful environment. Most people did not know what really goes down there. Though I had a poor childhood, the mistreatment at the group home had a more adverse effect on me. I was not the only victim—we all were.

Regardless of where I was taken, I still felt deserted and imprisoned because nowhere felt like home. In addition, each group home had its challenges. For instance, one is usually vulnerable to bullying by the other girls. Therefore, you had to stamp your authority, otherwise you would become a slave.

If truth be told, there is always someone whom everyone was scared of, and as a newbie, you are most likely going to be subjected to their mistreatment. So, after getting registered, I took my time in finding out who the linchpin was, and once I spotted the person, I knew I had to make a statement. I had learned from my past and was tired of being taken for a ride.

This was my biggest group home yet and I found out that we had to have our meals in a hall. After investigating, I found out who the linchpin was; a girl named Ashley, and from experience, I knew that she and her gang would already have a plan for me, so I was really nervous, conscious and suspicious. During dinner, I sneaked with my dinner tray to meet Ashley while she was eating her food quietly, and without warning, I slammed it on her face and continued to hit her with the tray. Everyone was staggered!

It was my first night, but I had to do something. She had not done anything to me yet, but if I wasn't proactive, I may be taken by surprise or even wake up the next day in some deep sh*t. Predictably, as I hit her, we started tussling and I saw blood all over but I didn't care whose it was, I just continued hitting her, trying to show her what I was made of so no one would mess with me. Yet, inside, I was overwhelmed with fear and anxiety.

After they separated us, the authorities had to evict me, saying I couldn't stay there because I was bound to cause them more problems. I had challenged their linchpin and the group home mustn't have two masters. That very night, I was taken elsewhere. Due to this bad report, no group home wanted me because I was labeled notorious. However, for those who truly knew me, like Judge Frusciante, they laughed knowing that I really didn't have the nerve for all that. They knew I only reacted out of fear to protect myself. Soon after, a group home finally accepted me. Meanwhile, I tried to get in touch with my mum and dad but neither of them were anywhere to be found.

Now, because I despised the idea of being in a group home, I made up my mind that I was going to leave. So, I packed my stuff secretly and absconded from the group home, convincing myself that I could cope on my own. Since I had nowhere to go as all my friends either stayed with their parents or in other group homes, I lived on the streets for the first few days.

When I could no longer cope with the cold outside, I started visiting my friends to stay with them all day while they fed me. However, when it was nighttime, I would have to leave because I couldn't sleep at their homes. So, what I often did was go to their parking lot to check if anyone in the neighborhood left the car open so I could sleep in the backseat. Needless to say, I slept in people's cars at night.

On one occasion, I was at a friend's place and when it was dusk, her mum asked me to leave so I could get home before nightfall. I couldn't narrate my plight to her, nor did I have any intention of returning there. So, as I left, I remembered they had a laundromat outside that could be used. Hence, I slept on top of the dryer because it was so warm.

After a week of living like a fugitive, I was at a gym trying to sign up when my name got flagged, and before I knew it, the police had arrived. As they interrogated me, asking why I left the group home, I narrated the whole ordeal, going on to threaten them that if they returned me there, I would commit suicide. That's how bad I hated the place. Nevertheless, the police, left with no choice, ignored my plea and took me back to the group home. As I returned, my face was covered with shame like the prodigal son, and the reality was that I was back to the pit of hell.

Years later, when I was sixteen, I met this guy named Caleb (real name withheld). His kindness and caring nature made me endeared to him, and in no time, Caleb and I began to date. He turned out to be better than I thought such that he would always provide my needs, and this made me feel like the only girl on Earth. Gradually, my self-esteem began to develop as he showed me my worth.

Call him God-sent and you would be right. I felt safe with him and thus, I always yearned for his company. So, I decided that I would always leave the group home to spend days with Caleb. Although they had a policy whereby if anyone goes missing for three days, the person would get a strike (meaning one would be confronted and punished by the Judge who is more like one's parent), but I didn't care.

For the first time, I had found solace in someone and nothing was going to hinder me from being with him. So, I came up with this plan to avert the consequence: I'll pack my things and go stay with Caleb for two days in a hotel and then return on the third day. This became a routine, and no one could hold any allegation against me because, with such a strategy, I didn't break the rule and never had to face any problems with the Judge.

Nevertheless, each time I left, the staff would start backbiting about me, calling me a whore and stripper and even when I returned, they wouldn't cease calling me names. On the contrary, I was dating someone who made me feel loved and luckily, he was financially stable, so I wasn't bothered about their insults. I just ensured that my things were locked lest they be stolen. Not even the staff was trustworthy.

One day, I went out and got my kinky twist hairstyle done at an African shop. Afterwards, I returned to the group home. Lo and behold, when I woke up the next day, I found out that my hair was cut. I was thunderstruck! How could a human being do this to me? Why is there so much hate and envy in this household? I thought. I was soaked in tears and had to call Caleb to explain my ordeal to him. He cheered me up, asking me not to worry and assured that I would have it replaced. He kept his word because the next day, I had it done again.

On one hand, I was glad that I had made a comeback statement, but on the other hand, I wasn't satisfied that the perpetrator just went scot-free. Filled with rage, I swore to myself that I would retaliate. A few days later, while everyone went to school, I stayed back at the group home and I went to everybody's closet and started bleaching their shoes, beds and cutting shirts and strings.
I didn't even care about their reaction. I just wanted to prove a point that I am not one to mess around with. When they all returned and saw the entire mess, there was a commotion. They all rushed towards me, trying to beat me but, luckily, the staff came to my rescue, grabbing me away from the scene to save me from them, otherwise it may have been terrible. Nonetheless, in my mind, I had gotten my pound of flesh.

Soon after, Caleb bought me a brand-new Toyota Yaris. I couldn't believe my eyes; that good things could happen to me. It felt like a daydream because all my life, no one had ever given me a gift. I was filled with goosebumps. So, at seventeen, I was now in glamour and everyone at the group home was stunned as this became valid proof that I was, indeed, a whore. Still, Caleb never relented in showing me love. He made life worth living for me and was my source of joy after being abandoned.

As a result, I totally submitted myself to him.

Yet, despite everything he did for me and the gifts he often showered me with, he never attempted to have sexual intercourse with me. How surprising! I became worried thinking it was absurd for a man to have a lady at his disposal and not want to take advantage of her, after all, that was the impression I got when I was initially molested. Several nights, we'd be at different hotels and while on the bed, I'd be thinking to myself, Why isn't he touching me?

To date, I cannot tell why. Perhaps he was too busy, or he just wanted to prove to me that he genuinely loved me. However, I noticed that even the other guys I hung around with at that period never tried to take advantage of me. It later became very obvious that they sincerely cared about me, or perhaps God had me covered.

One night, I hung out with a friend of mine and we had a falling-out with some guys. All of a sudden, one of them recognized me even though I had never seen him before and he was like, "I ain't fucking with Caleb's girl," and once others heard the name, they all dispersed, saying they didn't want to get into trouble. My friend turned to me and said, "Who the fuck is Caleb?" I was speechless.

Meanwhile, I had also noticed that each time I walked on the streets and tried to communicate with people, they instantly started trying to avoid me. When I probed further, I'd hear stuff like, "You are Caleb's girl and no one talks to you." After much investigation, I found out that my boyfriend was a drug dealer. Wow! So, while people were respecting me out there and telling me about my boyfriend, I didn't even know his true identity. One day, I confronted him and, surprisingly, he did not even try to deny it. Instead, he went ahead to ask me, "How do you think I got you the car and all those other things I lavish on you?" I was taken aback and then I replied, "I don't know, I just thought you worked hard."

Nonetheless, I admired his honesty, and since he did me no harm, I remained with him. During this time, I was struggling in school such that I had dropped two years behind my mates and a lot of factors were responsible. Most notably was the fact that the people who mattered to me had condemned me, especially my mother who kept reiterating that I was dumb, would not graduate and would not amount to much in life. Because faith comes by hearing, I eventually believed her words and it ultimately became my reality. School wasn't my priority because, in my head, I wasn't good enough. I had resigned to my fate of being a nobody and I felt dating a drug dealer was even a privilege.

One afternoon at school, one of my teachers, Mrs. Beverley, called me out of class, sat me down and revealed how I've been missing classes and stating the consequences of not being able graduate with my mates. I concurred by saying, "Perhaps it'd be better if I dropped out instantly and consider school later in life."

"Do you really want to finish high school?" She confronted me instantly and I burst into tears. After questioning me, I revealed to her that I'm not smart or good enough to be educated. She felt pity for me and decided that she would assist me. However, there was a policy that prohibited teachers and students from staying together. Still, Mrs. Beverley took the risk, working out a strategy on how we could study together.

Her plan was to ensure that she assisted me in working hard to see if we could reduce my outstanding classes at school to one year. So, she would give me lots and lots of assignments. Interestingly, I took them to Caleb and he would assist me with it in a jiffy. It turned out that he was good at math, which explained why he was so good at drug dealing. He would take his time to explain everything to me for hours. I'm really in good hands, I thought.
On the other hand, my teacher at school helped me sort out my other issues. Soon after, she came up with a new plan and made me promise to keep it a secret. Her strategy was, after school hours, she would pick me up at a particular junction and then drive me home where we would go through the schoolwork together. Every day, she ensured that we studied for at least four to five hours.

Right after that, I'd sleep in her house while she took care of everything else. She would feed me, wash my uniform and prepare everything I needed for the next day. The next morning, she would drop me somewhere close to the school, then I'd just take a stroll down like I was coming from home on my own. For the next six months, she perfectly assumed the role of a mother for me. In retrospect, it appears that my teachers were used by God to comfort me.

However, just when I thought life was beginning to smile upon me, I got hit with some bad news. Caleb had gotten arrested by the police after getting caught. Goodness gracious! My only love and companion! He was hereby charged to court for drug dealing. In spite of everything, it was during that period that I learned the whole truth about him. I only knew he sold drugs when, in fact, he was a drug lord. So, I had been dating a drug lord? Oh my God!

After being raided, it was discovered that he had money and drugs stacked everywhere in his house from the rooftop to the ground. As a result, he was sentenced to 40 years imprisonment. Back when we hooked up, it was always at one hotel or the other where we would lodge and have fun for two days before I returned to the group home on the third day. We had driven to his place on a few occasions, but I never slept over. I would only step in for a few minutes or just remain in the car waiting for him to return, so I really didn't know much about him. Nonetheless, it was heartbreaking that life had, again, taken someone who had become a great companion from me. More so, being incarcerated dashed my hopes of seeing him again. How sad!

Nonetheless, I took consolation in the fact that I was doing well with my studies and I became even more focused since school was all that I had left. Shortly after, Mrs. Beverley fetched me out of class one day, and I was perplexed because she wore a straight face. She showed me my transcript with everything I had submitted and revealed that, by some twist of fate, it appeared that I wouldn't have an outstanding year, but would be graduating along with my class set. I was puzzled! How is that even possible when, not too long ago, I was two years behind? In the twinkling of an eye, I would be graduating that same year!

After deliberating back and forth, she encouraged me to keep working hard as there certainly was a possibility that things may turn in my favour. A month before graduation, my mates were already getting their gowns and caps. Then, an administrative staff came to me for clearance so I could get mine. Confused, I asked, "For what?" She replied, "You're graduating." Lo and behold, after verifications, it was confirmed to be true. I couldn't believe it but, somehow, Mrs. Beverley's words were coming to pass.

A week before my graduation, my principal called me into her office to inquire if I had any more work to submit. After turning in the rest of my work, she greeted me; "Congratulations Tiffany, you are graduating." I stood in front of her crying my eyes out in disbelief. On graduation day, everyone was shocked to see me in the gown. Even when my name was called, I realized how unhappy people were with my accomplishment because I saw the reflection on their faces. Then again, I couldn't blame them because even my heart was racing a thousand times per minute as I felt it was all a daydream. I kept thinking to myself, how could this happen to me?

On top of that, they started calling out names for honours in different subjects, and all of a sudden, my name was announced as the best student in English language. Omg! I was so stunned to also win an award. So, while I was thinking I wouldn't graduate, I ended up graduating with two certificates. My graduation from high school was a huge success for me because everyone around me had written me off.

Prior to that time, I had managed to get in touch with my mum, and since I was shortlisted for graduation, I demanded her presence at the ceremony. I ensured that I sent her money for her bus ticket and every other thing she wanted. Yet, on the given day, my mother was nowhere to be found. I was so distraught that my eyes kept searching everywhere to be sure. Aside from my teacher, only my grandma and my female counselor at the time showed up to celebrate with me. Seeing how other parents showed up to celebrate with their kids made me even more sad. Why does this woman detest me so much? My heart ached. I knew Caleb would have loved to be there to cheer me on but, unfortunately, he was in jail. I felt so lonely.

Anyway, the feat reignited some level of confidence in me and I ended up going to Broward College. Soon after, I became increasingly dissatisfied at the group home since I didn't really have anyone who cared about me. Normally, one could age out at the age of eighteen or nineteen as long as one was independent. Though I was still seventeen at the time, I strongly believed I could fend for myself; after all, I still had my car and everything. So, I summoned the courage to pay Judge Frusciante a visit to discuss the possibility of leaving earlier than usual. After clearing his doubts, he yielded by granting me the right to age out of the group home. Freedom at last!

However, there was a challenge. I was labeled a juvenile delinquent due to my record (a juvenile record is potentially a criminal record), which meant that I was prone to committing a crime in future having had a past full of misdeeds. Truly, due to my behavioural problems, I went to juvenile a lot. In fact, my record was so bad that, when I was eighteen, I had a long list of misdeeds.

Technically, in Florida, any wrongdoing done before the age of 18 cannot be held against you, but my juvenile record was so outrageous that it became a problem, and most of it was juvenile battery. With the possibility of it affecting my future since I could be deprived of working for the government or in hospitals, I hired a lawyer and the battle began. It was no easy ride with the probation office as it took a long period of time. Nevertheless, after a year, my juvenile record finally got expunged.

At the age of 17, I moved into my apartment and got a job to foot my bills. Gradually, I learned to cope with life on my own. Then one day, the police came knocking on my door for further investigation on Caleb since I was his girlfriend. I became so furious that I threatened them because I was still a minor at the time. They quickly left when I mentioned that I was going to inform my lawyer. I was so upset because they were only adding salt to my festering sore.

The only person who managed to fill the void that my parents left in my life was gone. Although he kept writing me letters professing his undying love for me, I couldn't put my life on hold. To complicate matters, I realized that he still hadn't repented his old ways as he continued to push drugs, even in jail. So, I was forced to move on and get my life together piece by piece.

Chapter 4

BROKEN-HEARTED

"Sometimes, it's better to be alone...nobody can hurt you."
-Unknown

For every level in life, there comes another devil, which can be frustrating, but that's just how life is designed. So, what demon did I have to battle this time? Hang on....

After gaining my freedom, life did not suddenly become a bed of roses. No, it didn't. Although, by taking responsibility to work and pay my own bills, I had truly earned my independence, but self-reliance wasn't easy for a teenager. After getting my first job at a law firm where I was earning about $15 per hour, bills began to pile up so much that I had to keep working, working and working just to stay afloat.

As a result, working fulltime to pay my bills started affecting my schooling in the first year as I couldn't attend classes regularly. During that time, I met a young Jamaican named Norris P. I found him fascinating because he always had the neatest braids and, even more, a breathtaking scent. On top of that, he had fine brown skin and a muscular body, which made him sexy. So, we got along pretty well, and he helped reduce the pressure I was facing at the time.

After a while, we fell in love and started dating. Norris' presence made up for Caleb's absence in my life, and, more significantly, he had an impact in my life as he became the one who finally taught me all the domestic things that a mother ought to. Norris would teach me how to properly wash clothes, clean the home and prepare different dishes. To cut a long story short, he taught me all the Caribbean dishes that I know today. For this reason, I sincerely relished his company because there was always something new to learn from him.

However, I still felt dejected for not having a father or mother of my own, and, as such, I yearned for Norris to fill that void, but, unfortunately, he couldn't. This is owing to the fact that he also came from a dysfunctional family as he had a sour relationship with his father. Therefore, he also desired some things from me that I couldn't provide.

In other words, we were two broken people who sought for healing in each other, and this led to our relationship becoming toxic. Having realized this, I tried quitting the relationship on different occasions, but he would always react negatively. Yet, the red flags kept coming to indicate that we were heading nowhere.

Once, we were together and I answered his phone call, knowing it was from a female, and as a result, he snapped and he hit me, and this, in turn, brought out the beast in me such that I began to break windows and go crazy. While a good relationship ought to bring out the best in the couple, ours brought out the worst in us. We were shattered and we knew it, but we still held on, scared to let go. Nonetheless, the relationship only kept getting worse, and I was becoming fed up.

I remember calling him one day to inform him that I was done and no longer interested in the relationship. Then I hung up the phone. He called several times, but I refused to answer his call. Twenty minutes later, he howed up at my house and started yelling, "Tiffany, open the door, open he door." Five minutes went by and he was still banging on the door. So, I uriously went to the window and asked him to leave, telling him that my nind was made up.

As I left for my room to go rest, Norris punched a hole in the window to unlock the door. I became fearful and started running towards my room, out he got me before I got in and yelled at me, saying I cannot leave him. Somehow, we resolved the issue, and the next day, he paid my leasing office o fix the windows. That's how we kept going back and forth.

Nonetheless, our journey together ended when he got admitted into a college n Tallassee. On my part, I couldn't keep up at school, so I took some time off to face my life squarely due to the overwhelming bills. Although, along the line, I enrolled at a number of schools including the Beauty Schools of America in Homestead, Florida and the Robert Morgan Educational center to keep up with my growth and development.

Subsequently, I met Amaniax, an Asian American. He was 5 feet 9 inches tall, fair-skinned and handsome. As the managing director of two successful businesses, he was no doubt accomplished. He became my perfect gentleman because he was loving and caring to a fault. Take, for instance, though I had my own car, Amaniax would drive down to my house to take me to work and then, he would return after closing hours to drive me back home again.

He also made it a habit to come over to my house with surprise gifts, and I was always excited to see him. As if that were not enough, he would prepare my meals, open doors for me and put a call through often to know my well-being. He literally pampered me so much that I became head-over-heels in love with him, and the fact that he showed me so much respect made me always crave his company. Although, we had minor disagreements, as every normal relationship would, but aside from that, everything was just heavenly.

Seven months later, he proposed marriage to me, and I gladly gave my consent as I found no reason not to. Ever since I met him, I never had to worry about infidelity or anything whatsoever. Such was his uprightness that, each time I tried to support him financially, Amaniax would refuse saying, "No, you're the woman and I ought to be the one to provide and take complete responsibility." Such a man was rare to come by and even more was the fact that he also had an admirable physique as he always played soccer and I really loved to rock his body.

For the first three years of our union, things remained perfect. He still brought flowers home, whether there was a special occasion or not, and I kept drowning in his love. At the end of the third year, he brought up the idea of having kids. Now, prior to my marriage to him, I had informed him of the fact that I wasn't interested in childbearing due to my childhood experiences.

I didn't want any child of mine to go through anything similar and he was fine with the idea. So, when he brought it up again, I was disappointed because he knew the condition before marrying me and it wasn't as if I had changed the terms. Nevertheless, this caused a huge misunderstanding between us as he kept insisting on having children.
The next thing I noticed was that he began to take drastic steps by hiding my birth control pills, and sometimes, he may even go flush them down the toilet. He kept doing all kinds of silly things just to ensure that I became vulnerable for pregnancy. However, I rose to the occasion by taking alternative steps to ensure that I did not get pregnant.

After a while, his father got really ill and this bothered him a lot because he was beginning to lose enthusiasm in things he naturally found pleasure in. One day, he pleaded with me saying, "Tiffany, please, I really want my dad to see his grandchild before he passes away and I don't think he has much time left to live."

Those words pierced through my soul, and I felt touched. Knowing how much this would mean to him, I surrendered. I wished I had a dad I could live to impress, but since I didn't, I wanted to please my father-in-law instead. Shortly after, I got pregnant and after nine months and three weeks, we had our first daughter, Bella. Amaniax became so fulfilled and I saw a heightened level of ecstasy in him. I was overjoyed anyway, seeing that it only brought more joy and love to our home.

Nevertheless, my joy soon evaporated as it didn't take too long before tragedy struck. How? Amaniax's attitude started changing. His respect for me dwindled, he stopped caring for me as he used to and literally became complacent. Before Bella's birth, he practically idolized me, but he perhaps felt that since I had a child for him, I was now stuck with him, so he became relaxed and then began to unleash his demons.

For instance, we had a principle of being accountable such that we always revealed our whereabouts to each other. In other words, he gave me so much assurance that I never had to question anything about him whatsoever. Never! Even if I didn't hear a word from him in hours, I was rest assured that he was fine and had no cause for alarm.

Simply put, I trusted him like gravity. Then all of a sudden, he stopped carrying me along in his proceedings and began to do things on his own, feeling there's no reason to go the extra mile for me anymore. The flowers he always bought for three years of matrimony stopped during that period. I couldn't believe this was the same husband I married. I was perplexed!

While I was still thinking of a way out, he decided to play the same trick again: he started demanding for a second child. "Hell no, I am not doing it!" I reacted after his assertion. But once again, he became insistent and I couldn't cope with him nagging, so I resorted to taking my birth control pills so I wouldn't become pregnant again. We've just had a fresh baby and I wasn't interested in having babies back to back, I thought. I wanted us to at least take good care of Bella first.

How did he react? He started stirring arguments, and before I knew it, he became so disrespectful and would even become physically abusive. He could drag me or shake me sometimes such that I'd be wondering what had come over him. He became so touchy and would throw tantrums over trivial issues. I began to suspect that something was fishy. Therefore, I decided to keep a close eye on him, but it proved abortive because I never found any evidence whatsoever. Still, the mistreatment continued at home. Left with no choice, I remained his loving and submissive wife and I kept doing my duties diligently, not wanting to assume anything. On the other hand, I was beginning to become fed up with the marriage.

Meanwhile, since I was eighteen, I had given my life to Christ and I always had this hunger to grow spiritually. Thus, I enrolled for counseling and became curious to learn more about God and how to truly worship Him. I would read the scriptures on my own, including the Greek bible and do a lot of research, juxtaposing the King James Version with others. I also didn't allow my background to influence my faith. In other words, the fact that my mother was a Catholic was no sufficient reason for me to follow suit. So, I opted to choose my faith without being induced by anyone or anything.

Since I had a friend who was a Jehovah's Witness, I decided to attend their meetings at the Kingdom Hall, and I found it interesting. In no time, I became well-known amongst the congregation that my name often rang on their lips, but I wasn't ready to become a member just yet. I was only there to learn. Nevertheless, in that journey, something happened. I started noticing a lot of changes internally, not knowing that it was God who had actually been leading me into a deeper relationship with him.

So, when I initially got married, I ensured that Amaniax always worshipped with me at a church that was situated in a home around. Though he didn't like it because he had always been a member of the Seventh-day Adventist, I still forced him to because I needed to get my family involved in serving God.

Therefore, during those trying times in my marriage, I clung to God more. Then, one day in my confusion, I started communicating with God in the hallway: "God, I'm in this marriage and I have no grounds to leave but I feel something is going on that I am unaware of. I love this man and I've given him a beautiful daughter, but I feel something is not right, yet I have no proof. Lord, whatever it is, please bring it to light. If this is not the man for me, let me know and whatever you want my life to be, just do it, I'm all yours now."

Guess what! That same week on Friday, I was in the kitchen preparing a meal when I heard a knock on the door. I went to the door and opened it only to find a lady with a protruding belly, obviously pregnant, requesting to see my husband. I informed her that he was still at work and then I asked who she was.

"I'm sorry but he's been ignoring my calls and I've been trying to reach him for months because I need to talk to him." She replied.

"What's going on? Are you family or what?" I asked.

"I'm pregnant by Amaniax. He gave me money for an abortion, but I couldn't risk my life, and I've been trying to reach him to tell him that I couldn't do it." She answered.

I was still trying to internalize her words when I suddenly saw my husband approaching right behind her. What a coincidence! I thought. It was quite bizarre for him to return so early at that time of the day. What appalled me even more was that he was carrying some flowers with him. Earlier that day, we had an argument and I had complained about his new attitude and all the things he had stopped doing. So, it appeared that he had thought it over and he wanted to make it up to me or whatever, I couldn't tell.

As soon as he saw her, the flowers dropped from his hand and he rushed at her yelling, "Get away from my wife, get away from her, you're a liar!" Then he turned to me: "Get into the house and don't listen to her."

I was like, "What's going on? How can a girl with a big belly claim that you are responsible for her pregnancy and how did she even find where I stay, huh?"

All the while he had been disrespecting me at home, I had seen nothing because, there and then, this was the height of disrespect. As if that wasn't enough, she came knocking and stood there with audacity.

"I don't know, I don't know." Amaniax responded.

"What do you mean you don't know? You used to have me in the parking lot, waiting for her to go to sleep." the girl cuts in.

"Oh my God!" I exclaimed. This must be a daydream, I thought. She further explained how my husband would sneak out in the middle of the night just to hook up with her to have sex and they had been on that routine for a number of months. So, not only was my husband involved in infidelity, he went to the extent of having unprotected sex, putting my life at risk in the process when he could have at least used protection. On top of that, he had the nerve to bring her to our apartment.

I took a close look at the girl. She was looking so filthy and I shook my head, lost for words. Instantly, I called my Pastor because I needed someone to talk me out of doing something nasty lest I commit murder. When I narrated the whole scenario, he was left astounded. Afterwards, he explained, "Tiffany, you can either forgive him and move on or you can leave the marriage. However, if you choose to leave, it has to be on good grounds, which you already have, but before you do, be sure the baby is his."

So, I confronted my husband: "If her baby is yours, this marriage is over and I'm leaving."

My husband's response was a shocker: "You can't leave me, who is going to pay your bills?"

In other words, he was saying, I have you in this beautiful house, I got you a car, I'm paying all your bills and buying everything you need. So, who is going to pay your bills? You're not leaving because you can't do without me.

My heart sank when I heard those words. Yet, I had to swallow the bitter pill that I truly couldn't do without him after all, I didn't have anywhere to go. I didn't have a family to go back to or any relative to turn to. In other words, I was now in a danger zone. "Lord, what am I supposed to do at this point?" I broke down.

Since I had nowhere to go, I reluctantly swallowed my pride and stayed back. Without a doubt, I was really unhappy, and my matrimonial home now felt like the group home—a prison. The veil that concealed my husband's true identity was now removed, and it was evident that I had been betrayed.

In my mind, I was done with this traitor, but I had to remain with him because I was simply helpless. Now, I understood why he insisted on having kids at all cost—to enslave me and unleash his true character because Bella was barely five months when I got hit with this blow. That night, I lay in my bed, heartbroken, choosing to remain in the marriage especially for the sake of my daughter.

Now, I have this gift of discernment such that I often have dreams that give me insights. So, miraculously that night, I dreamt that Bella grew up to marry a man who also cheated on her and, as bad as she wanted to quit the marriage, she opted to stay simply because I had stayed in mine. Due to that decision, Bella suffered in her marriage. Immediately, I woke up. I felt so sad knowing what the consequences of my staying would be, but on the other hand, I was glad because that gave me the conviction I needed to leave that marriage lest Bella follow in my footsteps. Besides, I knew he wasn't going to repent due to his arrogance, and I had a prophecy to back that up.

Although, before I found out about his secret, I had made up my mind not to have any more kids with him since his behavior changed. So, when I found out about his promiscuous nature, I stopped giving my body to him. I have no problem being humble and submissive to my spouse, but if this is mistaken for weakness and his attitude affects the home, I would have to do what is necessary.

My job as a wife is to assist him in building a home, but when my husband is going astray, it's my duty to get him back on track. So, once I noticed Amaniax's behavior changed, I tried to draw his eyes to it, but he wouldn't listen. Rather than being happy that he had a helpmate who was there to checkmate him, his ego came in the way and he began to feel envious as though we were in a competition. On the contrary, we were supposed to be teammates complementing each other but he hated the fact that I was right and he was wrong.

Given his arrogant nature, I was left disappointed that he could even stoop so low to have sexual intercourse with a lady with no education, no standard or anything. To date, I still wonder how he managed to find such an ugly lady so attractive to go bed with. In fact, when I filed for divorce and we got to court and people saw her, they burst into laughter that the judge had to order that there be some decorum. I was so embarrassed.

Yet, even more shaming is the fact that two of his close friends who were also married also had sexual relations with this particular lady. This was brought to light after investigation as she couldn't identify who in particular was responsible for her pregnancy. That further revealed the kind of company my husband had been keeping. However, after they all got tested during a DNA test, my own husband emerged the shameful owner. How disgraceful!

Moreover, I later found out that the pregnant lady wasn't the only woman my husband had been sleeping with. Why me again? I pondered. I was so upset that life had hit me yet again. Is it that good things do not last or they aren't just meant for me? I thought. I had married a wealthy man who gave me everything yet, somehow, thorns had to come up with the roses. Left with no choice, I had to leave him to save my pride. So, I moved out of his house, and later on, the court declared us officially divorced. That's when my problems kicked off.

Instantly, I felt the weight of the world on my shoulders because I had given up a life of comfort in which I didn't have to work at all for a life on my own as a single mum who now had to take absolute responsibility for everything and my kid like a widow. Yes, a widow, because he died in my heart the moment I found out he cheated on me.

To complicate matters, he still had the nerve to say to my face that I couldn't make it without him, feeling that I would tolerate his immoral behaviour because I already had a child with him. Meanwhile, I had informed him at inception that I had only one rule that mustn't be breached: my husband must be faithful to me because I cannot cope with infidelity, and even if I had six kids, I would still leave.

Consequently, I took life by the throat working at two different jobs to stay afloat. In fact, I was working day and night, and thus, I had to hire a babysitter named Carmen. I felt like I had failed as a mother because I was leaving my only begotten child for someone else to nurture when I ought to still be nursing her since she was only six months old, but if I didn't do that, we were both going to suffer because, even with two jobs, I still struggled to maintain a roof over our heads, provide food and pay the numerous bills.

Luckily, Carmen turned out to be an angel as she was really kind and supportive, and she raised Bella till she was two. If truth be told, she is the most excellent babysitter I have ever had. On certain occasions, I would go to her place to see my baby and practically sleep on her couch because I was pretty exhausted from work. Yet, it was a rollercoaster of struggles because there were times I starved from having no money to even eat.

On one occasion, I broke down, regretting my decision to be separated as I had to endure back-to-back black outs at home because I couldn't afford the light bill. I thought my faith in God would make life easier, but it didn't. Nevertheless, the good news is that those dark moments of my life strengthened my relationship with Him, and despite my busy schedule, I created time to attend church every Sunday and it recharged my spirits ahead of the new week.

So, even though I had no light at home at the time or couldn't see light at the end of my tunnel, I had a feeling that everything was going to be alright. Amidst all the issues, God said to me, "If you can fully surrender to me and

trust me, I would order your steps and sustain you through your struggles."
I thought to myself, Why not? What do I have to lose?

I started by fasting for two hours every day, and though people tried to downplay the sacrifice, it was a whole lot for me at the time due to my workload at my two jobs. Overtime, I enrolled in more spiritual exercises. I prayed more, attended bible classes, listened to gospel songs and also abstained from sex. Soon after, I prayed for a new husband who would support and love me, but God made me realize that I wasn't ready since I hadn't healed or let go of the grudges in my heart.

In all honesty, I was still shattered because I held onto my past and it made me resentful and depressed. Some days, I never wanted to get up from bed. Other times, I couldn't eat because I would be reminiscing on my predicament, which would make me lose my appetite, and even when I tried to forget the past, the sight of Bella would spring them back to life.

God further said, "Tiffany, you don't even love yourself and you need to learn to. In fact, you loved your ex-husband more than you loved yourself and even me, your Creator." This hit me down my spine because it was absolutely true. Hence, I started practicing self-love and working hard to detoxify myself of every negative emotion.

With the aid of therapy, I was gradually able to let go of the traumatic experiences I had endured during my childhood with my mother. I kept working on my mental health, and steadily, I fared better. I would visit places such as the cinemas and the beach, and this habit turned out to be helpful. I would also read self-help books and watch YouTube videos on how to attain emotional healing. Soon after, I learnt to meditate—something I had never heard of prior to that time. In the third year, it was perfectly integrated into my system as a way of life—to date, I cannot do without it. So, I continued this recovery process till I eventually came through.

Meanwhile, as I worked on myself, I noticed Bella started acting strange. Out of curiosity, I inquired what the problem was, but she kept mute, scared of my reaction. After pleading with her to see me as a friend whom she could trust with her issues, she revealed her worries over not having a father and how she's in dire need of one. She further explained that, at school, all her mates have fathers but she's the only one who doesn't. Knowing that her school was predominantly populated by white kids, I could feel her pain.

This put me in a vulnerable position. I couldn't adopt a father or date any random man just to fit into the role of a father for her. On the other hand, I couldn't return to her biological father because he was utterly irresponsible and wouldn't give her a befitting upbringing. So, I was completely clueless.

More disturbing is that she reminded me of my childhood trauma, and I felt miserable that I had subjected Bella to the same situation I faced. Although Amaniax's family kept in touch and sometimes sent money for Bella's upkeep, that couldn't make up for his absence because he totally abandoned us, never bothering to call or check up on us to know how we survived. Not much different from my biological father.

They say, whenever you fall, make sure you pick something up. Thus, I picked up a lot of vital lessons from my broken marriage, and they have made me a better person. One mistake women make is marrying men just for the benefits they can get rather than for love. That's a disaster! Love cannot be traded for anything. Beyond luxuries, you deserve unconditional love. Besides, luxuries do not prove the authenticity of true love. Never go into a relationship for the wrong reasons or you will live to regret it.

In addition, love or attraction is not enough to marry someone. I learned this great lesson the hard way as I made a grave mistake by marrying Amaniax because of the affection with which he showered me. Get this straight: there's more to marriage than affection. You have to deal with your spouse's lifestyle, personality, habits and values, and if they are not right or do not align with yours, there is going to be a problem. Love and attraction are important, no doubt, but there are other virtues that make up the equation to make it fruitful.

Another thing is, most men do not understand the power they possess. For example, men were created first and were given dominion over everything. To put this into perspective, a child may argue with the mother, but once the man says, "Stop that!" The child automatically listens because of the authority embedded in him. Sadly, most of them use their power negatively or use it to abuse women because they do not understand its essence.

Moreover, some men feel challenged by their spouse's success, and rather than work as a team to complement one another, they begin to see their wives as a competition. How immature! Men are builders and providers while women are helpers and homemakers, and both parties must work hand in hand to raise a good home. Without good homes, kids are raised to become menaces to society because charity begins at home. Furthermore, a man must lavish his wife with love to raise a good family. That's why John Wooden said, "The best thing a man can do for his children is to love their mother."

There must be love and vulnerability. In fact, I love it when a man can share his fears and deep thoughts with his spouse. I respect men who can tell women how they feel, even if they are falling out of love. It would have been better if Amaniax confronted me by telling me he was no longer finding me attractive. I would prefer that to disrespecting me by cheating in marriage. However, I look back today, grateful for taking the bold step to leave because he apparently wasn't the right man for me, and a broken marriage is better than a broken life.

Chapter 5

OUT OF OBSCURITY

"Life can only be understood backwards, but it must be lived forwards."
-Soren Kierkegaard

The philosopher Aristotle was right when he said life cannot be lived and understood simultaneously. I mean, I can relate to this because I lived the most part of my life in utter confusion as there were scores of unanswered questions in my heart. As a result, I've constantly engaged my mind wondering why the dreadful events of my life happened the way they did. Still, it seems like, as I'm leaving one pain or challenge, I'm heading for another.

Nevertheless, of all the blows my life has been dealt, my mother's attitude and absence hurt me the most, and it continued to amaze me. Though my childhood experience made me question if she was truly the one who carried me in the womb, I knew in my heart that she was my biological mother.

Despite the fact that she gave me away, years after, I still yearned to have her back in my life. So, I desperately searched for her, but all my efforts proved abortive. Later, owing to my persistence, I found her on Facebook, and after much investigation, I found out that she lived in Atlanta, Georgia. I was so elated.

When I finally got to speak with her, I was over the moon that I had reconnected with my mother, but I could feel that she hadn't changed much. Still, I overlooked all that and kept in touch with her, after all, I wasn't that little kid she could mistreat or verbally abuse anymore. Overtime, nothing changed as I noticed that she only maintained our relationship just to foot her bills.

She would call me every week claiming that she didn't have food or money to pay the light bills. As a matter of fact, each time she called, it was because she needed something, and because I didn't want to lose her, I kept meeting her needs on top of mine. However, when I noticed that this attitude of hers had become a pattern, I intimated that I couldn't continue to pay all of her bills because it was beginning to affect me since I was still growing myself and also had Bella to care for.

However, out of sentiment, I didn't want to turn my mother down, so each time she called, I would find it hard to say no to her. Hence, she continued to make demands till it got to the point where I had no more money to give her. At that juncture, because I was helpless and felt sympathy for her, I resorted to taking my company's money. I did this for months just to provide for her.

One day, the manager at my workplace called me into her office, informing me that she was aware of how I have been misappropriating the company's resources and she demanded an explanation. I felt so ashamed. So, I confessed to her that I did it just to cater for my mother's needs, but that wasn't enough to vindicate me or buy me a second chance. I was hereby fired! It was so sad, but I had to accept the consequences of my actions.

Afterward, I explained my plight to my mum over the phone, emphasizing the fact that I lost the job because I took risks just for her and she shouldn't be expecting any miracle afterward. To my amazement, she had no words of encouragement for me. In point of fact, she acted as though she didn't care. There and then, it dawned on me that my mother did not give a hoot about me.

Again, I felt so disappointed. After all my efforts in trying to extend the love she deprived me of, she could not reciprocate the love out of empathy. What could I have done to my mother? What is it about me that she hated? Apparently, if I had ended up in jail, she wouldn't have acted any differently.

After that conversation, she never called to see how her daughter and granddaughter were faring. Two years later, out of the blue, she called, and before she could mutter anything, I felt she wanted something again, but she shocked me by asking after Bella instead. She didn't ask for anything at all. I was amazed! Afterwards, she started keeping in touch to check up on Bella.

As a result, I thought it wise that, since my mother had turned a new leaf, it would be nice for her to meet her granddaughter. So, I mapped out a plan for her to travel down to see my daughter. Therefore, I sorted out her greyhound ticket, though, I was quite strict at this point as I told her that if I was bringing her to see my daughter, then she had to be consistent as opposed to just popping in and out like she was fond of doing with me. More so, Bella was still a kid and such an attitude could have a negative effect on her. My mum gave me her word that she would pay her role diligently.

Seven months after that first experience, I made arrangements for her to visit a second time. Nevertheless, she left me disappointed again because, after that, she disappeared into thin air as I heard nothing from her for over a year. So, I made up my mind not to entertain her again because I didn't want my daughter to keep asking for a grandmother who showed no sign of affection or concern.

Having tried over and over to rebuild the relationship between us and it was clear that it wasn't working out, I redirected my focus to my lifelong desire: my father. Since I was a kid, I always had this burning desire to know him. Who was he? What did he look like? Wasn't he aware that he had a full-grown daughter? These questions saturated my mind. As I pondered, I remembered that I once heard he was from the island and had joined the military at a young age.

There was a company called United Services Automobile Association (USAA) for those serving or had served in the United States Armed Forces. Though I barely knew my father, I knew his full name and date of birth. So, it happened that one day, something drove me into action, and I called up the USAA company saying that my dad was in the military and I wanted to open an account.

"What's your dad's full name?" The customer care personnel asked.

"Patrick Whittaker." I responded.

"What state does he live in?" She inquired further.

I became perplexed because I had no idea. Instinctively, I quickly grabbed my phone and searched for his name on Google. In a jiffy, three states popped up and, immediately, I remembered that my grandma once mentioned that his wife stays in Virginia, so I decided to stick with that.

"Virginia!" I replied.

"Okay." She said as she typed on her computer system.

Amazingly, it turned out to be true as he still lived in Virginia. So, she kept typing while she went on to read out his details to me in a bid for me to confirm the information.

"Yes, I've found him with this address...right?" She asked after reading it out.

"Yeah." I consented like I already knew all that.

Then she proceeded by reading out his phone number and, immediately, I wrote every piece of it down, assenting to her.

"Okay, I will put you right under him now and open your account. Here are your discounts that you can get under your father... Thank you so much and please extend our regards to him; we thank him for serving his country." She concluded.

I was taken aback! Because, with little to no effort, I had my father's entire details jotted down on paper. After ruminating on the whole scenario, I decided to dial my father's number. However, it was his wife who picked up.

"Hey, I'm Tiffany Whittaker. I want to speak with Patrick Whittaker." I said.

"He is at work right now but I'm his wife so you can talk to me." She responded.

Obviously, she didn't hear my surname, or she just didn't read any meaning to the fact I was bearing the same surname. So, I went further to say, "Well, I'm his daughter and I just want to speak to him." A silence ensued…perhaps she was trying to process the information.

"Hello!" I interjected.

Then she responded, "I'm sorry but I think you got the wrong number."

At this juncture, I reconfirmed my dad's name, going ahead to read out his house address and ended by saying that, since I was calling Patrick's phone number, I was absolutely sure of who I was calling.

"But Patrick doesn't have a daughter." She cuts in.

"Ma'am, Patrick has a daughter. In fact, he has three daughters because he has two other daughters aside from me." I insisted.
"How do you know this is the right Patrick?" She asked. So, I narrated to her how my dad was stationed in Miami in 1989, and as I recounted, she confirmed my words because he was stationed there for four years.

So, she said, "Let me call you back when he gets home."

I thought it was a trick to dismiss me until I got a call four hours later. Surprisingly, it was from the same number, but now it was my father on the phone. Finally! I thought.

His masculine voice brought relief, and while I was drowning in the euphoria of hearing from my father, his response sent shock to my spine. "Hey, you got the wrong person. I don't know who you are, and I've never heard of you. So, you got the wrong person." My father yelled.

"Hold on, hold on, give me a sec." I quickly interjected, not wanting to give up easily.

I quickly placed the call on hold and dialed my Grandma's number. As she picked up her phone, I said, "Hello Grandma, I've got Patrick on the line and either he is lying to me or you have been lying to me."

"What's going on?" Grandma asked.

"Patrick is on the other line and he is saying he's not my father." I answered.

"What! C'mon, merge the calls and let me speak to him." My grandmother yelled.

I merged the call and, instantly, my grandmother snapped, "Patrick, Patrick Whittaker? You don't remember Tiffany? You don't remember who I am?" Then she went ahead to mention his father and mother's name. She also cited specific events that happened.

"Oh, oh, now I am beginning to remember," my father said.

At that point, I became infuriated. "Oh, so you knew who I was from the beginning, but you just wanted to mess with me, right? You trying me?" I yelled.

"How could you do that? How could you deny your own daughter? Do you know what this girl has been through?" Grandma interrupted.

"You're a liar! You're a liar! So, you got a daughter and for over twenty years, you never bothered to tell me?" His wife started yelling and crying in the background.

I got more furious and added, "Ma'am, it's not only me."

"What do you mean, 'it's not only you?'" His wife asked.

"I'm not his only daughter. He's got me, Erica and Jessica. It's all three of us."

"Oh, I don't think so. Or maybe he's not aware of that." She responded, trying to cheer up herself.

"He's been playing you, ma'am, because he just spoke to Erica and Jessica yesterday; in fact, he's been talking to them for several years. I'm the only one he blanked out. You check his phone and you will find out that he's been sending money to them for years. He does everything for them. I'm just the only one he's counted out." I insisted.

I guess she went ahead to check all his phone messages because afterwards, I started hearing things breaking and she kept screaming, "You're a liar! You're a liar!"

"What do you want from me? You have already grown. I have nothing for you and want nothing to do with you." My father yelled and dropped the phone.

I was horrified! All my life until that day, I had prayed, fasted and yearned for this golden moment. Yet, my biological father not only denies me, but goes ahead to warn me to stay away from him. I was devastated. This was the very first time I had an encounter with him, and he chooses not to identify with me.

He clearly meant his words because that was the last time I ever heard from him. Even when I called him afterwards, he never picked up. I even sent him pictures of my daughter on Facebook Messenger to make him realize that he's now a grandfather, and though he read the message, he didn't respond. That further hit the nail on the head that he really wanted to have nothing to do with me.

I had always learned that he was extremely deceptive to the extent that he got another woman pregnant about the same time as my mum, despite having a family in Virginia. In fact, it happened that, while he was dating my mum, he would drive down to her office after closing hours to take her home. Then, along the way home, he would also pick up the other woman he was having an affair with, claiming she was his sister and vice versa. I heard all that but I still wanted to meet my dad so he could prove otherwise to me. Nonetheless, here I was, getting my own shocker.

Although I am still entitled to some benefits that he can't exempt me from as his biological daughter, I have never set my eyes on him to this day. Whenever he travels, I get notifications about his whereabouts and some financial benefits, and even when I don't need them, I have to exhaust them because that's all I have.

Yet, these benefits are nothing compared to having a relationship with one's father. I only saw pictures of him and heard his voice over the phone, but I never got the opportunity to meet him. It can be painful when you are an orphan but it's even more heartbreaking to have your parents hale and hearty and yet, they deny you as a child. You are an orphan all the same.

Soon after, my dad's wife called me and started asking if I opened an account under my father. I instantly questioned her right to query me. After all, neither my mother nor I ever got a dime from him. So, why in the world would she question the fact that I got peanuts from him? Could that make up for the fatherly love that I had been deprived of? I even dared her to do something about it like take the matter to court because I knew it would backfire at her since the government detests parents who do not take care of their children.

However, I later forgave my dad, not because he deserved it but because I needed to be free from bitterness. I knew that I needed it because resentment is like drinking poison and expecting the other person to die. So, I freed myself from the hurt unforgiveness would have on me. Though I truly wanted him in my life, I couldn't force him to accept me. Nevertheless, I strongly believe that he will come back one day begging, but at that time, it may be too late. Perhaps the day he leaves the world, he will reflect on his life and regret the fact that he never had a relationship with one of his daughters.

Afterwards, it became clear to me why my mother was always bitter and why she acted the way she did to me. If my father could boldly deny me, then he must have really hurt her back then. Thinking about it, if I had never known my father, then he must have rejected my mother when she conceived me. These mysteries led me on another quest to decipher the genesis of every anomaly.

Although my mother had a fair upbringing, she also endured trauma as a kid. I nean, she suffered similar challenges to mine when she was young. During her childhood, she and her sisters were playing one day in their courtyard when suddenly, this stranger who was obviously drunk comes to her and says, "I'm your father."

My mum responded by denying his claims. Still, he insisted and went further to mention her full name, birthday and other details. Then he reiterated to her: "I'm your dad." My mum became puzzled that a stranger could know this much about her. If he was saying with conviction that he was her biological father, then it was probably true. Suddenly, my mum burst into tears feeling deceived to believe that her stepfather was her biological father.

So, my mum's sister ran into the house to inform my grandmother about what had transpired, and the drunken man's story was confirmed to be correct. To explain further, the truth is, my grandma had nine kids with this particular man (my mum's stepfather) and only my mum didn't belong to him. Interestingly, my mother was also her first child. In other words, my grandmother also had a sour relationship with my mother's biological father who suddenly appeared from nowhere.

Consequently, my mother became distressed, and since then, her life never remained the same. She developed mental health problems and stopped talking to everyone, feeling betrayed and different from others. Though her stepdad treated her extra special and provided everything she needed, not wanting her to feel like an outcast, but that proved to be insufficient when the cat was out of the bag. Hitherto, the relationship between my mother and my grandmother had gone bad.

More significantly, my mother was about seven when this ensued—about the same time my own trauma began. To complicate matters, even my grandmother dealt with trauma herself because her mum (my great-grandmother) died when she was also seven and her dad (my great-grandfather) went on to abandon her afterwards.

So, if you do the math at this point, you could decipher that there's been a negative pattern in my lineage. Let me expound: my great-grandmother had nine kids, my grandmother had nine kids, and now, my own mother also has nine kids. In addition, not only did my mother give birth to me out of wedlock but her first three kids were also born to three different men who she wasn't married to.

Despite falling victim to my dad who deceived and denied her, she still subjected herself to two other men who merely got her pregnant because none of them fully committed or married her. As if that weren't enough, she got married to another man and went ahead to bear more kids for him. How ridiculous! I know she may have been lonely, but even at that, did she have to bear six more children in addition to the three that she already had and could barely cater for? Intriguingly, I am the first child, just as my mother was the first child of my grandmother.

To cut a long story short, it's like pain and suffering going from generation to generation. In other words, there were a lot of mystical things that were orchestrating our realities, but I've been the only one to break that jinx and rise above the odds. My mum later furthered her studies by obtaining a masters in theology, but I know it was all a cover up because she is yet to overcome her trauma. My mother has a habit of acting as though she is happy, and she has this incredible ability to make people think and believe what she wants. Nonetheless, deep down behind the scenes she is not happy.

To make matters worse, my mum was indulging in self-destructive habits that only worsened her condition. For instance, I never witnessed my mum smoking or doing drugs, but I later found that she was smoking cigarettes so bad. Today, we seldom communicate, but whenever she decides to reach out to me or come over, it's the same old story: she simply needs something from me, but be that as it may, whenever I can assist, I make sure I do not deny her anything.

While she has the proclivity to think that she's taking advantage of me, I do what I do for her so as to see her and be sure that she's perfectly okay because, despite all that's happened, I still love her wholeheartedly. Sometimes, she may begin to boast that she raised me well, but I never fail to remind her about my childhood and then she becomes defensive.

I remember one time when we were still kids, mum told Josh and I that she would be taking us to a place, and that if we cooperated, she would buy us whatever we desired. All we had to do was act dumb when they asked us questions, irrespective of what they asked or did. As naïve as we were, it sounded nice to us. On getting here, we played along such that when the agencies started questioning us, we gave no reply. As promised, Ma bought us things and we were so happy. Little did we know that she had signed us up for social security and had started collecting disabled cheques on us as if we were truly disabled. No wonder she asked us to act dumb. What a mother!

Fast forward to the time I was working, I often noticed that I was restricted in my working hours. One day, social security contacted me, informing me that they had been sending cheques to my mum for years because I had a learning disability called Special Learning Disability (SLD). I was shocked, but there and then, I recalled the occasion and it became clearer to me. I had to prove to them that I was mentally fit and independent, and that was when they stopped sending the cheques. I felt liberated because I had finally broken away from the limitations that were crippling me, and I could eventually maximize my potential.

Sadly, my brother, Josh, couldn't stop the cheques because he truly needed it at the time. As kids, Josh used to be my closest sibling even though we usually fought because he would do things to hurt me but that was out of child's play. Josh loved animals such that he could take lizards, cut them open and do all kinds of amazing things with them. However, today, a lot of my mum's decisions and actions have also affected him.

Many times, we drown in turmoil, wondering why our lives are the way they are, and as we ponder, we only become more confused. Even when we come up with answers, it scarcely fills the soul's void. However, sometimes, we just have to pause and reflect to dig deep because you can't see your reflection in running water—you can only see it in still waters. How we got to where we are entirely depends on the past, that which has been lived and not the present.

Digging deep enables us to make sense of the world and our place in it. That's why Steve Jobs said, "You cannot connect the dots looking forward; you can only connect them looking backwards." More importantly, amidst the confusion and uncertainties in our lives is an opportunity to draw closer to God. In fact, that's the major essence of it. For example, it was Hannah's barrenness that drew her closer to God, and it was David's insecurity that took him to greater depths with God.

Interestingly, He knew you even before you were formed, and He knows your past, your present and even your future. So, if you are buried in obscurity and dining in perpetual confusion, seek God's guidance so He can bring you out of your situation. He has done it for people in the past, He did it for me and can do it for you too. It wasn't just my research or reflection but His guide. He took off the veil from my face to answer the questions lingering on my mind for years. Simply put, He pulled me out of obscurity so I could live my life with clarity.

Chapter 6

BEHIND THE SCENES

"If I have seen further in life, it is by standing on the shoulder of giants."
-Isaac Newton

It was John F. Kennedy, the 35th President of the United States, who said, "We must find time to stop and thank the people who make a difference in our lives." So, before I bring down the curtains on this book, I need to appreciate the people who have worked behind the scenes to make me who I am today because behind every public glory, there is always a private story, and considering the gory experiences that I've had in my life, I wouldn't be standing tall today without these people. Sit back and relax as I introduce you to the beautiful people who have added colour to my life.

In the foster care system, I met Marsha who was also admitted there. We turned out to be best friends, especially as we shared similar circumstances. However, we later fell out when she became green with envy that I had a good relationship with Caleb (the drug lord). In that process, she tried luring him to bed just to have him to herself (which she later succeeded at).

When I found out, it was so heartbreaking that I did not need a soothsayer to tell me to cut her off. On the flipside, Marsha had a sister named Raquel Broom, and she was a great fighter and well-known at the foster care such that no one tried to mess around with her or anyone she cared about because Raquel wouldn't think twice before smacking the person. So, as the door to my friendship with Marsha closed, the door to a fruitful relationship with Raquel swung open.

Raquel became my ride or die friend. We did naughty things together, and if anyone messed with me, she would ensure that she dealt with them. As a result, I always felt safe and loved with her. Sadly, as the years went by, life happened, and we lost contact for donkey's years that I had already forgotten we used to be friends. One day, out of nowhere, I got a message on Facebook from Raquel and she was so eager to reconnect with me. At first, I was hesitant to reconnect with her because I was now mature and had dropped the bad habits we had as teenagers. In other words, I was judging her by the past and wary of bad eggs coming back to corrupt me.

After thinking it through, I decided to give her a chance, only for me to find out that she was now a completely different person much to my amazement. When we connected on the phone, she sounded so refined, positive and keen on meeting with me. As we kept having our chitchat, I discovered that she lived only about two hours away. Hence, we had a rendezvous and afterwards, it became a habit to have dinner together.

Since then, Raquel has made a huge impact on my life. In point of fact, she became the one who taught me the nitty-gritty of business. She literally sat me down and coached me on how to start my limited liability company. She also gave me a practical guide on how to get it licensed and how to run the business. She's been totally involved in my business to date.

Ultimately, she fit into the role of a business advisor whilst still remaining my good friend. Today, Raquel is happily married to a Muslim with a child, and despite being business savvy, she creates time for her passion, which is cooking (especially vegan food). She is also an advocate for her community as a black woman. She ensures that she patronizes and indulges in anything to support its growth. Most significantly, she has been a great motivator to me, and despite her achievements, she's still a humble individual. I agree with the words of Zig Ziglar, "A lot of people have gone further than they thought they could because someone else thought they could." In due fact, I have gone further in life because of Raquel's presence in my life. It's essential that we have people who would lighten our burden and make the journey of life fulfilling.

Due to my past experiences, especially in my dealings with back-stabbing people, I hardly associated with people because the past kept haunting me. Yes, I have colleagues, acquaintances and the likes, but as for my inner circle, I almost had none. Nevertheless, it marked a big step in my development when I realized that no one is an island, and if I truly wanted to go far in life, I had to go with people as opposed to walking alone. However, I still maintain only a few friends. Audriana Edwards happens to be my best friend today, and I will narrate why.

While I was still married to Amaniax, my ex-husband, we moved into a luxury apartment, and shortly after, I bumped into a neighbour of mine named Audriana. She stood with a kid and was also pregnant at the time. As we exchanged pleasantries, my spirit instantly connected with hers because she had a positive aura. In no time, we got along and became good friends. We would visit each other and spend quality time together, and sometimes we cooked dinner together. It seemed we had known each other since childhood.

In the long run, when life hit me through my divorce, Audriana played a pivotal role in my life as she literally became my comforter, encouraging me each time I wept over the situation. When I needed someone to talk to, Audri was ever-ready to listen and her words were usually: "Girl, you better move on, God's got you. So, just move on." She lightened my burden and helped me get over those trying times. Though, as friends, we had ups and downs in our relationship to the extent that we sometimes argued and fought, but we always ended up staying stuck to each other because we valued our relationship.

Over time, she became my accountability partner such that, every morning, we would speak over the phone and would even talk for up to an hour. We would deliberate on issues such as our progress as well as our struggles, and then give each other pep talks concerning our daily and weekly goals. Through our relationship, I learned that no two people can have the same perspective.

In other words, though friends and lovers may cherish themselves and have a sustainable relationship, challenges will always arise in the form of misunderstandings. In fact, it is healthy to have them sometimes, but bridges should not be burnt over temporary issues. People who truly value their relationship should learn to tolerate and overlook the differences between them. A true friend is someone who thinks that you are a good egg even though they know that you are slightly cracked. I love Audriana so much. We are like one soul dwelling in two bodies.

After a chronic period of loneliness following my divorce, I decided to move on and give myself a chance to mingle again. So, I got on eharmony, an online matchmaking site for singles. There, I met this guy named Jack. He had very light-brown eyes, short, curly hair and the footballer kind of body. He was soft-spoken, and we got along pretty well, becoming great friends. Later on, he convinced me to move to Jacksonville since he resided in a three-bedroom house with his daughter about the same age as mine.

Of course, at this time, we had already started dating, so I obliged him because, from day one, I knew without a doubt that he truly loved me, even beyond the way I felt for him. Though we made a pact that I would pay half the rent, it didn't take long to realize that our being together would only be short-term because living with him exposed me to some of his bad habits that I couldn't condone such as smoking, gambling, etc.

I was very honest in my dealings with him as I always complained about his lifestyle and how it wasn't good for my daughter, yet he persisted in his behavior. Things were quite tough for me at the time and I just needed to get by, so, in the meantime, I endured the inconveniences. I gave him my all, but I just never saw a future with him.

As a matter of fact, it appeared as though we were on a contract because we shared the bills in the house. I became desperate to leave, so I gradually saved up money for a new apartment. However, all hell let loose when I informed him one day about my plans to leave as soon as possible. He wasn't pleased with the idea and hat led to a heated argument.

Suddenly, he grabbed me by the neck and slammed me as though we were wrestling. Perhaps he felt that by putting his hands on me, I would become scared to leave and stay put. On the contrary, I went haywire like the incredible hulk such that the moment I got up from the floor, I began to demolish the house. I smashed the television in the sitting room and broke every glass I could see.

I dashed to the kitchen, grabbed a knife and destroyed his furniture. I damaged the refrigerator and dismantled his closet. He was shocked! Seeing how I went ballistic, he became scared and immediately called the police. In a few minutes, they arrived, and with their intervention, I became calm. After careful interrogation, I narrated how he violated me, and in the twinkling of an eye, he was bundled and thrown into jail.

As a result, I had to leave the house. I couldn't stand being in that negative atmosphere or living in that house because it had become toxic for me. That's the main reason I was skeptical about keeping relationships—because toxic people tend to bring out the worst in me.

The money I had saved up was only a part installment and an application fee, and upon arrival to the apartment complex that I wanted, they informed me that I would be needing far more than what I had. It was disappointing, but then I remembered that, upon leaving Jack's apartment, the police mentioned that I could stay in the Hubbard House, a shelter for women who suffer violence.

I moved down there with Bella and things went well during the first few days. They fed us well and took absolute care of Bella whenever I left for work, but over time, we both became increasingly uncomfortable. To complicate matters, sometimes my belongings would go missing, which made me even more anxious to leave. During that period, Audriana kept in touch to comfort me. Nonetheless, I was desperate to leave and I worked tirelessly for two weeks uninterruptedly to raise funds for a new apartment. I was really stressed out, but I didn't mind as I just wanted a breath of fresh air.

I notified the authorities at the Hubbard House that I was leaving, and they asked if I could grant an interview with the executive team, so I obliged them. Two days before my exit, I attended the meeting and they basically wanted to inquire why I was leaving because I was the first person to ever demand to leave the shelter in the shortest time possible. They were curious to know why and if I was truly ready to move on. I acknowledged them for being hospitable and supportive, and I mentioned that I had learned not to settle for someone like my ex-boyfriend with bad habits. Conversely, I narrated the fact that I had some challenges at the shelter, and I needed to move on since I had already secured an apartment.

After the meeting, one of the team crew by the name Ann Sabbag approached me. She gave me her complimentary card and asked for my phone number in return. She mentioned that she would love to keep in touch from time to time. She kept her word because, two days later, I got a call from her, and we spoke at length as she inquired how I was coping. Initially, I was so cautious because she was too good to be true as she always appeared to be positive and happy.

I felt she had an ulterior motive. Perhaps she wanted to know more about my background or get something she needed. So, I gave her a hard time such that I often ignored her calls, but that wasn't enough to discourage this dogged woman. Rather, she continued to call me over and over, leaving me countless messages to the point that I became really bothered as to why she was so desperate.

Out of provocation, I picked up her call one night and started questioning her, "Why are you always calling me? Why are you so particular about me when no one else cares?"

She replied, "Tiffany, I have nothing against you and have no ulterior motive or negative reason. When I heard about your story from your childhood, I was inspired, and I made up my mind to be your friend. I just want to support you and be that friend you can always count on. Seeing who you are now as a mother and a fighter, I want to be in your inner circle."

I was speechless because her words were heartwarming. I had no one to look up to as a mother or support system and here was someone fighting for that place in my ife despite me rebuffing her. Hitherto, Ann Sabbag, the stranger I was avoiding, turned out to become my mentor, my driving force and, most of all, a mother figure. After about a year, her impact on my life became so enormous that I began to adore and idolize her.

She practically walked her talk. When everyone turned their backs on me, Ann's arms were ever-open to receive me, whether I am right or wrong. I have called her seeking her assistance at the dead of the night—sometimes 12 or 1am, and still, she never shunned me. Rather, she was always willing to give me her listening ears.

As a matter of fact, one particular quality I appreciate about her is that, even when I am wrong in a situation, she will subtly tell me about my flaws and then, without my permission take responsibility in fixing the mess. To date, she never judges me, and as a result, I am never scared to be vulnerable with her or show her my scars. Ann runs a business that promotes healthy living, and though her job can be so demanding because she often travels, she creates ample time to call and visit me. On some occasions, we even have lunch together. On one instance, she begged me to accompany her to the beach. I was so mesmerized because, as an accomplished person, I never felt worthy of hanging out with her. It's been five years now and I have no regrets whatsoever for letting her into my life.

I almost gave up on life, but Ann was always there to come to my rescue. Even at my lowest point with my face to the ground, she would always show up and her presence always meant the world to me, and I would be rejuvenated to fight my battles. She would listen to me pour out my heart and always cheer me up. Her words of encouragement, attitude and everything have immensely contributed to who I am today. In essence, without Ann as my mentor, I may have lost it along the way but her presence in my life has made me go on to defy the odds.

After I left the Hubbard House, I got a job at a company called Martin Gottlieb, and during my early days, I was assigned a mentor named Nicole Edwards to train me on the job. During that exercise, Nicole and I really connected, and after a week, we had lunch together, which helped build our bond. Shortly after, we had dinner again, and before I knew it, this lady who was my superior at work became so endeared to me. Afterward, she invited me over to meet her parents and I obliged her. It didn't stop there as that led to us doing a lot together, including attending church together.

One day, she invited me to a girl's night with her college colleagues and because she had been an angel to me, I couldn't refuse her. We had an enthralling night out, and just when they were about to disperse, the girls decided to round off by sharing their deepest gratitude. When it got to Nicole's turn, all of a sudden, she became emotional and burst into tears.

I was stunned! What could be wrong that I wasn't aware of? As words escaped her lips, she sang my praises: "Girls, I'm thankful to God for meeting Tiffany. She's an angel. She's got a beautiful soul. I know that I've known you girls for years and you are my family, but Tiffany means just as much as you all mean to me even though I just met her. I am saying this because I really want you all to know that. More importantly, I want her to know that I love her and she's now my sister."

At that point, I was filled with goosebumps and tears soaked my eyes. I had never been so eulogized before in my entire life. That day marked a whole new beginning for Nicole and me because for her to publicly declare her love for me amongst her peers, she truly deserved a place in my heart. I can never forget those words and moments.

I remember the day I met her mum, Mrs. Deborah Booker. She completely accepted me and made me feel comfortable like I was her biological daughter. In fact, as I left for home that very night, she specifically asked me to text her when I got home. When I didn't, she called me saying, "Didn't I ask you to call me when you get home?" I chuckled and she went on to ask about Bella, instructing me to bring her over to the house during the weekend. I was dumbstruck. What a mum!

Even when we finally had time to talk elaborately and I told her about my background, she shrugged off the sad tale, telling me not to be weighed down by it because she already sees me as one who came from her womb. She meant it, too, because she never changed towards me. She always showered me with love, love and more love. As if that were not enough, her husband, Mr. Corwyn Booker (Nicole's dad), whom I now call dad, was no exception because, in point of fact, he filled the void in my life that my biological father left. He was God-sent because he was custom-made for me such that whenever I needed anything, he wouldn't mind walking a thousand miles just to get it for me. Simply put, my wish is always his command.

It was so miraculous how everything I lacked was given to me on a silver platter. After all, God gave me the family I never had in Mr. and Mrs. Booker. I deem them to be my adopted parents and I can boldly credit a huge part of my success to them. Whenever I have challenges or emotional issues, they are always at my beck and call. Even my daughter, Bella always yearns to be with them and they, in turn, have taken her to be their granddaughter.

Although the baggage from my past wasn't all gone, Nicole made it her duty to ensure that I keep evolving. It was quite challenging for her at first because I was rigid. Still, Nicole would never give up. Instead, she persisted in ensuring that I was purged of all my bad attitude. For example, I used to have bad habits such as throwing things on the floor, but Nicole transformed me, and it now irks me to see people do those things. In other words, her good company influenced me a great deal. My daughter has also benefited from our relationship.

Plato said, "People are like dirt—they can either nourish you and help you grow as a person or they can stunt your growth and make you wilt and die." Interestingly, the aforementioned people have done the former to me, and my story wouldn't be complete without due credit to them. I have come to realize the fact that my true family are not those whom I am bound to by blood but those who love me and have been a pillar in our lives.

Above all, I appreciate Abba, my Heavenly Father, who stood by me through thick and thin. At times, I felt cursed and thought I was doomed for failure. I even attempted suicide by swallowing a whole bunch of pills, but somehow, I ended up vomiting. Today, I know it was the Lord's doing as he has clearly shown that he had a plan for my life. God's tests are now my testimony, and if I had not gone through those storms of life, I may not be living a fulfilling life today—and I would not have been inspired to write this book. The fact that I was able to overcome my struggles and affliction should give you hope, healing and the inspiration to overcome yours.

I believe God never wastes a hurt because he surely knows how to use it for your good. Just trust Him and allow Him to lead you, and one day, your mess will become your message with which you would inspire people who have gone through similar situations. It won't be easy. In fact, tears fill my eyes as I share my story but God insisted that I do this as sometimes our agonies are a revelation of God's mission to us because when we go through an affliction and overcome it, He wants us to help others going through that same hurt by sharing our heartbreaking story.

Interestingly, you could as well build a ministry based on your painful circumstances and its lessons, thereby becoming a model for others going through a similar situation. For example, it could be that you are going through that heartbreak because God wants you to help heartbroken people in the future by sharing how you overcame your heartbreak experience. That's the more reason you must not let your situation define or shatter you. Instead, let it strengthen you.

Today, I do not only reside in one of the best apartments in Florida but I also manage a thriving business called Tiffany Lush & Co. and we pride ourselves in combining secrets of the old world with that of the new, creating an array of sensual soaps and body products. In other words, I've grown from a child who was forsaken and couldn't cater for herself to a CEO who now pays her employees, and I particularly feel elated about this because I defied all odds. How?

In the United States, the number of children living in single-parent households continues to rise and the rippling effect of this is that those children are five times more likely to live in poverty and commit crime; nine times more likely to drop out of school and twenty times more likely to end up in prison. So, for me to break out of that cycle is a huge blessing coupled with the fact that it seemed that I had a generational curse in my lineage.

Asides that, I struggled because of the negative statements I constantly heard during my childhood which were my formative years and it was difficult to eradicate it from my subconscious mind. Yet, through God's grace and mercy, I conquered. And to further astound you, out of the thirteen of us who ended up at the group home, only three of us have turned out well. When I visited Miami recently, I found the rest of them living on the streets. As if that wasn't enough, they all have an average of eight kids as single mothers while one of them has now passed away from drugs. It feels so sad!

I was born not to make it and my life could have been worse considering these circumstances, especially when I was divorced and jobless with my child, living hand to mouth but I fought tooth and nail for my breakthrough. Now, I do not have to lean on any man for financial support to pay my bills. My daughter is also enjoying the best life there is, and we live happily.

Interestingly, Amaniax, my ex-husband, now calls and has been trying to win me back into his life but I have gotten over him, and as much as I want a father figure for Bella, it's not enough of a reason to go back to him. Besides, he went about impregnating women such that he now has five kids by three women after proclaiming that that would be my fate, thinking I would be at the mercy of men to survive. Apparently, he unconsciously cursed himself because everything he decreed would happen to me bounced back on him. Everything!

To complicate matters, he tried reuniting with the lady who got pregnant by him. In the process, he got the shocker of his life as she got pregnant again by a close friend of his and they eventually got married, making him lose on both sides. Beyond doubt, Amaniax got a taste of what he did to me. Nevertheless, what baffles me the most is that, despite all this, he still hasn't turned a new leaf to this day. In other words, he is yet to learn his lesson, so I am glad I made the right decision to leave, and my actions have been vindicated.

Success is a journey, but I surely won't stop aspiring for higher grounds. My experiences may not be the worst there is, but it was enough to ruin me if I didn't fight for my life. So, before you dread the clouds in your life, remember that it also has a silver lining. More so, when a bowl is broken in Japan, rather than throwing it away, it's put back together with the cracks being filled with gold. This emphasizes the fact that your life cannot be broken or damaged beyond repair.

In other words, you must embrace your pains, sorrows and imperfections so that you can create a more beautiful piece of art in yourself. It's the same way broken tiles are used to make beautiful designs. Besides, if delicious meals can be made from bitter leaves, then why can't you make a beautiful story out of your supposed terrible circumstance?

There's a giant in you and perhaps your hardship is trying to awaken it. Life's a mixture of ups and downs, and while our good times bring us comfort, our bad times build our strength and character. So, irrespective of how much your life has been shattered, I want you to know that you are more than a conqueror.

CONQUEROR OF A SHATTERED HEART

Ever yearned for love like a baby wanting breast milk? Ever been in the throes of loneliness? Ever dreaded your existence that you attempted suicide? Certainly, I have. I know what it means to dine with despair. I know the pain of a sour life.

I was denied by my father, discarded and sold out by my mother, mistreated by my guardians, molested by my therapist, betrayed by my spouse... Not even the depths of your imagination can decipher the gravity of my suffering. No doubt, life is full of victims, but it is also full of victors because, through it all, God intervened, and I wrestled till I snatched victory from the jaws of defeat.

Conqueror of a Shattered heart is the story of an innocent girl who put back the broken pieces of her life and filled it with gold to create a beautiful masterpiece. You think your life is broken beyond repair? This book would shatter such belief...

Made in the USA
Middletown, DE
19 September 2021